HUMBLED BY THE JOURNEY

LIFE LESSONS FOR MY FAMILY ... AND YOURS

FOREWORD BY DAVID LAWRENCE JR.

HUMBLED BY THE JOURNEY

LIFE LESSONS FOR MY FAMILY ... AND YOURS

MIGUEL "MIKE" BENITO FERNANDEZ

With Martin Merzer

story farm

Humbled by the Journey: Life Lessons for My Family... and Yours
Copyright © by Miguel "Mike" Fernandez

All rights reserved.
No portion of this book may be copied or distributed without the express
permission of the author.

Published in the United States of America by Original Impressions, LLC. Design
and editing by Story Farm, LLC.

Library of Congress Cataloging-in-Publication Data is available upon request.
ISBN 978-0-9905205-2-8
Printed in China

Project manager: David Lawrence Jr.
Editorial director: Ashley Fraxedas
Book design: Amanda Bardwell
Photo editor: Christy Marks
Copy editor: Eva Dougherty
Project facilitator: Lourdes Martin
Production management: Tina Dahl

Photographs courtesy of Mike Fernandez. Additional images, Shutterstock.com:
p.25, Cheryl Kunde; p.34, M. Pellinni; p.67, IanC66; p.81, Moreno Novello; p.107,
Robyn Mackenzie; p.113, Francisco Javier Gil; p.115, Ander Dylan; p.121, Nattika;
p.133, Pecold; p.138 top, Marco Prati; p.138 bottom, Ashley Whitworth; p.149,
Sergio Gutierrez Getino; p.154 left, Mariyana M.; p.154 right, gresei; p.193 top,
villorejo; p.194 bottom, saulpaz; and p.230, tupatu76.

10 9 8 7 6 5 4 3 2 1
First edition, December 2014

FOREWORD
BY DAVID LAWRENCE JR.

Mike Fernandez and I are not exactly two peas in a pod.

For one thing, he's an exile, born in a country later beset by communism, subsequently and forcibly evicted from his native land. (My forefathers came over on the Mayflower.)

For another thing, I know of no one with more of a knack than he for making money. (That, to be sure, is not my strong suit.) For yet another: No doubt we've voted quite differently over the years.

Yet...

He reminds me of me. (That's not all good!) We both are burning a candle at both ends, seeking to be "thoroughly used up" in our lives, in the memorable phrasing of George Bernard Shaw. Neither of us is saving our energy for the next world. Neither of us is the surrendering sort.

We are both "naïve." Can that even be possible for someone who has made billions in business? Or someone who spent 35 years in the rough-and-tumble world of daily newspapering during its robust years? That naiveté gives us both headaches at times. But, it turns out, expecting good things from people works out well most of the time.

We both love where we live, and see Miami as a place that previews the America that could be — diverse and loving to be just that, a place where people learn to appreciate the humanity we have in common, a place where most of us want to welcome others and help them toward the "American dream," too.

Like me, Mike is incessantly curious. He's passionate about his family, his values, about his community and country, about being fair, about the big picture (and the details). He can't stand to see people mistreated. He gives, generously so, in ways mostly unknown — and prefers it that way.

This book is the self-portrait of a larger-than-life fellow who never acts like a big shot.

His is a story — told poignantly, accompanied by pain, humility and wisdom – of two journeys. One took weeks. The other is lifelong.

Mike affirms for me the truly important in this life. I have learned so much from him. You will, too.

David Lawrence Jr. retired from The Miami Herald after a 35-year career at seven newspapers as reporter, editor or publisher. During the past 15 years, he has devoted his energies to building a movement for "school readiness" and early learning.

For Constance and the family:
those who came before us and those who will follow.

PREFACE

BY MIGUEL "MIKE" BENITO FERNANDEZ

I am a reluctant and humble writer of this book, but do acknowledge that I seek to achieve two main objectives with it:

- To help my children and those who follow them understand our family's history in Cuba, our arrival and growth in our new homeland, and the challenges we faced and overcame — and to help others recognize and appreciate what truly is important in this life.

- At the same time, profits from this book will go to further the cause of building a "school-readiness" movement for children in their early years — knowing that 90 percent of brain growth occurs in the first five years of life, and knowing that the future success of our beloved country depends on children getting off to a good start in life and in school.

INTRODUCTION

HUMBLED BY THE JOURNEY

"There is a greater good. I know it.
I can feel it."

It is Day 32.

The blisters are healing, or maybe they've just become so natural, so much a part of me, that they evade notice. Most of the mountains are behind me now, but so is the sunshine, so is the warmth. I could say it's downhill from here, but it's not. Many mountains await on the horizon, and the rain and the wind and the cold promise to persist until I complete this journey.

This journey that serves as a frame of my life and of the man I have aspired to be. This journey that will inform the balance of my life. This journey that increasingly inspires me to share with my children, my grandchildren, my friends and my colleagues the full measure of what I have experienced and what I have learned during the wonderful and often astonishing life that I have been so fortunate to lead.

Three hundred and sixty-four miles behind me. One hundred and forty-four miles ahead. The journey across France and Spain is a pilgrimage that is endured — no, experienced — by more than 200,000 people every year, each for a quite individual, quite personal reason. It's called El Camino de Santiago, "The Road to Santiago." It's also known popularly as "The Way of Saint James." The Way is a route that can begin from any of several locations in Europe. Most often, it leads through France, over the Pyrenees mountains and into northern Spain, then westward toward the city of Santiago de Compostela. From there, a few march on toward the small town of Muxía on the Atlantic coast. In ancient times, the Romans called it Finisterre, "the end of the Earth." The Way has existed for more than a thousand years and it still attracts pilgrims from all over the world. I'll share more details presently, but for now know this: This journey is rigorous — and it is magnificent.

Also know this: I do it for sick children and for the staff at a children's hospital. I do

it for myself. I do it for reasons I barely can comprehend or even grasp, but I understand — as profoundly as anything I've ever understood — that I must do it. I must complete this mission.

Of Values and Obligations

My name is Miguel Benito Fernandez. For as far back as I can remember, everyone has called me Mike, and I like that. I'm 62 years old. I was born alongside a small road, in an apartment above a used-bottle warehouse in the town of Manzanillo, tucked into the southeastern corner of Cuba. I am proud of my Cuban heritage. At the same time, I am an American, through and through. I care about the community I live in and I'm grateful to the country that gave me a home. Many take the meaning of "home" for granted. I don't.

I am a son, a brother, a husband, a father, a father-in-law, a grandfather. I am a family man and a businessman. Others would say that I have been blessed financially — well beyond my expectations. I cannot deny my good fortune. I will not apologize for it, because I worked hard for it. I took risks for it. I made sacrifices for it.

But I sometimes find myself surprised by it. I prefer to remain behind the scenes. Relatively few people have heard of me, yet I have been called "wealthy" by the media. That makes me uncomfortable, but I suppose that it is true. It is true

Everyone calls me Mike, and I like that.

19

This map outlines the 508-mile walk from France to northwestern Spain. As you can see, I will be walking from Saint-Jean-Pied-de-Port to Santiago de Compostela. It will take between 40 to 50 days and perhaps 3 million steps to complete, but it will be worth every step just knowing it will benefit sick children and their families.

This journey
is rigorous
and it is
magnificent.

SANTIAGO DE COMPOSTELA

RÚA

CASTAÑEDA

O COTO-LEBOREIRO

LESTEDO

PORTOMARÍN

SARRIA

TRIACASTELA

OCEBREIRO

LAS HERRERÍAS

VILLAFRANCA DEL BIERZO

CACABELOS

PONFERRADA

MOLINASECA

RABANAL DE

PORTUGAL

FRANCE

LOYOLA SANCTUARY
SIDE JOURNEY IN HONOR
OF THE JESUITS

START
SAINT JEAN
PIED DE PORT

RONCESVALLES
VISCARRET
AQUERRETA

PAMPLONA

SPAIN

ESTELLA · PUENTE
LA REINA

TORRES DEL RÍO

LEÓN

MANSILLA DE LAS MULAS

EL BURGO RANERO

SAHAGÚN

CALZADILLA DE LA CUEZA

CARRIÓN DE LOS CONDES

FROMISTA

CASTROJERIZ

BURGOS

ATAPUERCA

VILLAFRANCA
MONTES DE OCA

VILORIA DE RIOJA

SANTO DOMINGO
DE LA CALZADA

NÁJERA

LOGROÑO

...AL DE ÓRBIGO

IRELAND   UNITED
           KINGDOM

FRANCE

MAP
DETAIL

PORTUGAL SPAIN

The Fernandez family at their Park City, Utah, home.

"They all love the snow. I prefer the sea and the warmth."

mostly, however, because of the richness of the life that I have lived and because of the blessings that God has provided for me and for those around me.

This is a wealth somewhat beyond measure. I mean this not in financial terms, but — of primary importance to me — I mean it in terms of the good that I've been permitted to accomplish. I consider myself wealthy not by what I have made but, rather, by what I am able to provide for others.

At the outset, let me say this as clearly as I can: I did not want to write this book. My most comfortable place is under the radar. But some of those whose opinions I greatly value — my wonderful wife, Constance, and my good friends Cesar Alvarez, David Lawrence Jr., Eduardo Padrón and others — prevailed upon me to do so. They believe that I have experiences and lessons, values and wisdom, to share. I'm not sure about that "wisdom" part, but I did come around to accepting their advice.

"I DO THIS FOR THE SAME REASON I DO MOST THINGS — IN HOPE THAT PEOPLE CAN BE INSPIRED BY MY EXPERIENCES."

So, here is the point: I write this book and share these thoughts at the insistence of those I most respect. I do it not for glory, not to massage my ego, and certainly not for publicity.

I do this for my children, George, Alex, Michelle, Michael and Cristofer, and for my grandchildren, Stella and Daniella, and I am sure for others to follow. I do it because *they must know and they must never forget that they are the*

A cool hat, traditional outfits — and big smiles.

Mami and Papi dressed for a festive occasion in eastern Cuban (Oriente Province) attire.

beneficiaries — and the representatives — of a family that over generations has sacrificed mightily and worked tirelessly on their behalf.

They also must know and never forget that they shoulder the burden and the privilege of carrying our family's values and obligations forward to their own children and to everyone with whom they come into contact. Always with politeness and gentleness.

I do this, too, for the same reason that I do most things — in the hope that people from all walks of life can be inspired by my experiences with friends and family, and in business, and in engaging in the good works that I've been fortunate to perform.

People often ask me why I do the things I do. This book contains the answer. We all are a product of our families and of our history. This is some of my family's history and this is my story, and I hope you find value in it.

I have a creed, a structure, that I inherited from my parents, Mario Antonio Fernandez and Lieba Fernandez Gomez, and within which I strive to conduct my life.

In the late '40s: On the right is Lieba Gomez, the mother of Mike Fernandez, in her growing-up years. Next to her is her aunt and beloved music teacher, Digna Eulalia Telarroja.

A horse was not
a luxury in our
family. I learned
the love of horses
from Papi.

More than six decades
together, and still hold-
ing each other. Morn-
ings at the Little River
Plantation in Havana,
not far from Tallahas-
see, Florida. (What
a coincidence in city
names!) Each morning,
Mami and Papi walk to
the stables to talk to
the magnificent Friesian
champions — Crusader,
Hendrica and Cor.

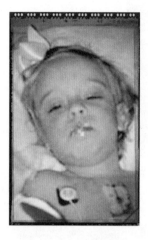

FAMILY FIRST, PRIORITIES IN LIFE: *"Meet my grand-daughter Daniella. She is the reason I first asked for support of my 508-mile walk from France deep into Spain in the fall of 2013 for the benefit of a children's hospital. Seeing the picture of this little angel placed a face behind the donations. At 19 months of age, Daniel-la needed open-heart sur-gery. She was in the good hands of the great doctors at Miami Children's Hospi-tal, a wonderful institution that I have supported in various ways for years, but still ... open-heart surgery, on a 19-month-old child, on ... my ... 19-month-old ... granddaughter."*

This is as close as I can come to expressing it:

I am spiritual in nature, but not particularly religious, if that is defined by attending church regularly, though I benefited greatly from my education and other contact with devout Christians — especially the Jesuits — and with Jewish people and others. Knowing this, someone recently inquired about my concept of God.

This is what I said: "To me, God is goodness. God is doing good to and for others. There is a greater good. I know it. I can feel it. And that is God, or, at least, godliness."

I don't understand how people can be meanspirited. I think people are naturally good. It's a lot easier to do something good than to do something bad. It's a lot easier to do something right than something wrong.

When we do something wrong, we know it — we try to justify it or rationalize it. When we do something good, we don't have to justify it. It just feels right. How can I help you? What can I do for you? It really isn't that hard.

"AND THEN IT CAME TO ME — I WILL MAKE THE PILGRIMAGE THAT I HAVE BEEN CONSIDERING FOR SOME TIME."

So I've learned through the years to let that goodness come through. Most often, this tends to express itself with children's healthcare and education.

Is that what I'm here for? Is that what I've been meant to do with my life, with the goodwill that I have earned?

I can't deny that the thought has occurred to me, especially when I see that certain look in a parent's eyes. I think we all have seen that look. I know that I've seen it far too often.

It's the look that says, "My child is ill — seriously ill. I have done everything I can imagine. What else can I do? There must be something. Tell me what it is, and I will do it. I will do anything. I will give anything. I will give my life and I will do this in an instant, without even thinking about it, if you will just make my child healthy, if you will just give my child a chance."

Yes, I've seen that look. I've seen it many times. Not long ago, looking in the mirror, I saw that look in my own eyes.

At 19 months of age, my granddaughter Daniella needed open-heart surgery. She was in the good hands of the great doctors at Miami Children's Hospital, a wonderful institution that I have supported in various ways for years, but still . . . open heart surgery. On a 19-month-old child. On . . . my . . . 19-month-old . . . granddaughter.

The operation was a complete success, and Daniella's heart now is fine. But I met someone that day in the waiting room, a mother of an adopted child. The woman also had the look in her eyes, and we talked, and I listened to her pain, her anguish, her sense of helplessness and desperation, and then it came to me: I will make the pilgrimage that I have been considering for some time — a 508-mile hike through France and Spain, through the mountains and valleys, the heat and the chill, the gentle and restorative mist and the hard and stinging rain.

"GRATEFULNESS IS A WONDERFUL GIFT WE GIVE OURSELVES. HONESTY IS ANOTHER, ALTHOUGH NOT ALWAYS WELCOME."

I will do this to raise funds for that woman and so many people like her — people whose ill children are in need of treatment and whose resources, both emotional and financial, are stretched to the limit. I will do this because God or circumstance or some power I cannot fathom has given me the ability and the resources, the reason and the urge to do it.

I will do this, and I will finish it. And, somehow, it will give greater meaning to my life and to the things I hold most dear: my relationships with my family and my friends and my community. My devotion to sharing blessings with others, particularly those in need. And, yes, to clear my own mind of the distractions of everyday life, to free myself to concentrate on what is good and right and proper. To concentrate on the sense of gratitude that has come to envelop me.

For, at the core of my being, I am grateful.

I've had my own health challenges recently, my own brushes with infirmity and

After Mass, in Roncesvalles, Spain, the priest asked only the pilgrims to stay. "Pilgrims, where is home?" he asked in Spanish, French, English and Italian. There were a dozen of us — each from a different country.

Cold, wet and tired: "It rained for days. Every step was difficult."

even death, so believe me when I tell you that I am grateful for the gift of today and for the gift of tomorrow and for the gift of yesterday. I am grateful for every day of life, for every interaction with everyone with whom I come into contact. I am grateful for the opportunity to share my blessings with others.

Gratefulness is a wonderful gift that we give to ourselves. Honesty is another, although it's not always welcomed. My wife tells me that I have no filter when I speak my mind, and she is right. That can be both a blessing and a curse. It is, in any event, who I am.

For me, there are certain principles that are not negotiable. Some of those principles are respect for others, and delivering a finished product to the best of your ability. When I see that someone is getting paid, I expect an exchange of capital in return for time and effort — not a haphazard effort and not a part-time effort.

Returning to the true and only purpose of this book, trust me when I tell you that I am grateful for the opportunity I now employ to share with you this journey — this journey not only through France and Spain but also through life.

I AM GRATEFUL FOR THE GIFT OF TODAY AND FOR THE GIFT OF TOMORROW AND FOR THE GIFT OF YESTERDAY.

Finding Deep Truths Along the Way

So, there I am, in northern Spain. It is Day 32. I'm more than two-thirds through this pilgrimage, but challenges remain. I have been mostly wet.

Horrendous rains and flash floods are predicted for the rest of the week. The mud is deep and seemingly everywhere. It is impossible to stay on the trail, unless one walks along the side of the road, but that is too dangerous. Worse than the rain is the wind. Even the long johns do little to help.

I have 14 miles to go before I enter the town of Sarria, which my daughter Michelle and I already reached earlier in the year, as this was the starting point for our original 62-mile walk to Santiago de Compostela. I should make that by the end of the day. If the weather does not improve, I will consider my journey complete, given that, between the two journeys, I will have covered the entire 508 miles.

In doing this for the young patients, their families, others in need and for the people I've met along the way, a notion — maybe a certainty? — comes to mind. It reoccurs when I recall the images of sunrises and sunsets, of mountains and valleys, of villages and towns, and the good people therein - images that now are engraved in my consciousness.

I remember a very special man at a fence in Mexico, a man named Eugenio. I remember a young lady from Brazil who desperately needed assistance. I remember the folks along this road in Spain. There was an old man, a goat farmer, who gave me fresh goat cheese and wished me a good journey. I remember another old man who, as I sat under his window to avoid the burning sun, offered a bottle of water and used a string to lower it and a banana to me. "Buenos días, amigo," he said. *Good day, friend.*

The notion reoccurs again as I consider the sum total of my life and how I have lived it and how I intend to live it.

"I HAVE BEEN TOUCHED BY ANGELS. I HAVE BEEN BLESSED. AND I HAVE BEEN HUMBLED BY THIS JOURNEY."

It is a thought that I have come to know as true in the deepest reserves of my soul and my heart:

I know that I have more than to which I am entitled, and I know that I have been placed in a position to help others, to muster the assistance of my family and friends, to convey my family's history and its values.

As if through a filtered funnel, my entire life has narrowed and clarified into this:

For some reason, God has put me in a position in which I can help others.

When it comes to God, when it comes to children, when it comes to their parents and to their doctors and to their benefactors, when it comes to my family and to my friends and to my business associates, I am but an intermediary.

When it comes to all this, I say with profound humility: I have been touched by angels. I have been blessed. And I am humbled by this journey, this journey through life.

* * *

Throughout my pilgrimage, I tried to stay in touch with the outside world as often as possible, mostly by sending emails at night and, more importantly, through Facebook. For that, I relied on a young lady from the children's hospital, Sara, who is a social media expert. Nearly every day, at the end of my walk, I sent her an email. She edited the notes and posted them on Facebook. This allowed followers of my journey to stay tuned into my progress each day.

Before I left my home in Coral Gables, the children's hospital gave me a stack of laminated cards that contained a picture of each child at the hospital, some terminally ill but all in poor health one way or another. I carried these cards in my backpack. At the end of each day, I dedicated that day's experiences to a particular child. I said his or her name and told him or her everything I had experienced on that child's behalf. Sometimes, I wrote an email to the child or to the family. Sara, back at the hospital, would make sure that the message was delivered.

Taken together, this material, which I will share with you in chronological order throughout this book, forms a fairly complete electronic diary of the pilgrimage.

But before we get started, I know what you're getting ready to ask. Here's the answer: I lost 21 pounds during the experience. Call it "Mike Fernandez's 32-Day Camino de Santiago Pilgrimage Diet Challenge." But I don't necessarily recommend it. As weight reduction programs go, surely there is something easier than this.

My e-mails from El Camino

AUGUST 3
While training in Utah

Never thought I would be doing this. This day, the steepness and boulders made it difficult. Did a total of 1.6 miles in three hours, and I could not take another step. Then, you think about a child going through chemo, and realize, what I am doing is nothing and it is by choice.

Mount Timpanogos, at 11,752 feet above sea level and the second-highest mountain in Utah's Wasatch Range, is majestic at this time of year. The person in charge of getting me in shape is a young Argentinian named Victoria and, like most of us, she, too, has a story. I hired her because she knows these back trails, but as the days went by, I learned that she has a daughter afflicted with cancer. Now that she knows the reason for my walk, she also has her heart set on my success. Regardless of the challenges that life has placed on her shoulders, she is a naturally happy person. She is my cheerleader!

"Before I could start my long walk in the fall of 2013, I needed to get in shape. That involved strenuous exercise with a trainer in Utah."

"Then, as I left for Europe and my son Cristofer left for school, we compared backpacks."

"We passed through every sort of landscape — not only hills and forests but also towns like this one. Our starting point was this main street in St-Jean-Pied-de-Port."

SEPTEMBER 21

Saint-Jean-Pied-de-Port, the day before Cesar Alvarez and I take our first step on the path — and learn that everything is 3 hours away.

Saint-Jean-Pied-de-Port ("Saint John at the foot of the mountain pass") is a walled, medieval town. Many European trails meet here as they head south, then west toward our final destination on El Camino. The fortified walls and towers, the narrow streets compel you to learn, appreciate and remember the town's history. My great friend Cesar Alvarez and I walked to the "Pilgrims' Office," where we registered for the pilgrimage and received our "Passport." This document is stamped at each of the locations where pilgrims spend the night as proof that they have earned a certificate of completion when they arrive at Santiago de Compostela.

At this time of year, there are relatively few pilgrims. The high season for pilgrimages is over, and mostly it is the more adventuresome who are beginning their journeys with us. High season for the more than 200,000 or so pilgrims who make this trip each year is between the middle of May and early September. That is the dry season, but also the warmest. In the Basque country of France and Spain, they have two seasons, summer and winter, and they literally come along a few days after each other.

Our climb tomorrow is the steepest of the 508-mile walk. It's 24.83 kilometers (about 15.5 miles) and it normally takes about seven hours. Because of my bad back and ankles, I will walk slower, but Cesar is with me for the next week and he may be carrying me part of the way. L-O-L.

CHAPTER**ONE**

DEPORTATION AND DISTRESS – EARLY LESSONS AND FORMATIVE EXPERIENCES

"You have to take care of those who come after you."

When you come right down to it, we are the sum of our genes, our families, the people we meet and who influence us, our experiences, our environments, and what we carry away from all of it.

It all begins, of course, when we are children.

Like any other child, I had dreams and fantasies, which, in my case, played out as I lay on top of the flat roof of our apartment, in a town beside a bay full of brackish, muddy water. The roof's tiles were made of red clay and they were flat, unlike the barrel tiles of neighboring homes. From time to time, I would hear gunshots in the nearby mountains, but this seemed normal, as I lived in a region of Cuba far from the capital. It was here that the bearded revolutionaries of Fidel Castro started their insurrection against the government of Fulgencio Batista. (It's the region where

"I was no saint. (Look at my eyes!) My sister Pili was, and is, a better person. Mami was our protector. Note the bullet holes behind us (even after repairs)."

most revolts in Cuba started. It is possible that my independent and non-compliant personality is a geographic gene!)

So, I was not bothered by the gunfire. I lay shirtless with my back against the cold tiles and I looked at the stars. I held my eyes shut for a few minutes to better see the stars when I opened them. Then, there they were, like lighthouses in the dark, each star almost touching another, yet millions or billions of miles apart. I knew my world was changing, and this was not the place for me, yet I never could have imagined where my journey in life would lead.

I was keenly aware, however, of where it began — with my parents, of course, and their parents, and so on, back through time, back through our family history.

My Father — The Entrepreneur, the Provider, the Protector

My father, Mario Antonio Fernandez, was born on January 19, 1928, near the small town of Campechuela, in the southeastern corner of Cuba. It was a good life, but a hard life. He was one of 15 children and resources always were scarce. By the time he was 10 years old, Papi was working fulltime in general stores run by his uncle.

"BY AGE 24, MY FATHER OWNED THREE OTHER SANDWICH SHOPS, A CAFETERIA, A BAR AND A JUKEBOX BUSINESS."

Between the ages of 14 and 19, he traveled by horseback every day across the countryside, three hours to work, three hours back again.

His uncle, Rodrigo, was a great mentor. Uncle Rodrigo taught my father the importance of savings. He set high standards and imparted a

Uncle Rodrigo: "My father's compass in his early years."

41

terrific work ethic. Living in the country, there were few places to spend money, so my uncle gave my dad only a small portion of his salary. The rest went into savings.

At age 19, my father told Rodrigo that he wanted to go out on his own. Dad was shocked when he learned that 90 percent of his earnings were right there, in the store's safe, waiting for him. With those savings, he moved into Campechuela and bought a bakery, which quickly grew until he sold it just a year later. By this time, he had met my mother in the nearby town of Manzanillo, and he bought a small sandwich shop there.

He was bitten by the entrepreneurial bug. By age 24, my father owned three other sandwich shops, a cafeteria, a bar and a jukebox business that operated in many locations. He was young and already respected.

In Manzanillo, my mother, Lieba, had been raised by her father, Benito Gomez Cespedes, and by her grandmother in a house belonging to her uncle, Juan Telarroja. As a child, I considered this man, my great uncle Juan Telarroja, as my grandfather, and I respected him greatly. To this day, I recall him as "Chi-Chi-Cha," the nickname I fondly bestowed on him. (My actual grandfather passed away only a few months after my birth.)

My mother, Lieba, had been raised by her father, Benito Gomez Cespedes.

It was an extended family, all living under one roof. One of the most significant figures in my mother's life was her aunt, Digna Eulalia Telarroja Gomez, a teacher of classical piano. From her, my mother inherited a passion for classical music. My mother was 17 when she met my dad, seeing him as a hard worker, a man who had a vision, an aptitude for business with a natural intelligence for financial management, and an impressive ability to judge the character of others.

And so, they married, and they began a family, and they built a life. I came along first, on July 24, 1952 (though the date recorded at the local courthouse was August 5, 1952). Then, two years later, my sister, Pilar de los Angeles Fernandez (Pili), was born. Meanwhile, my father built his business. Outside, however, in the country that we so dearly loved, pressures were intensifying, and trouble was approaching.

A Visit From the Milicianos

Christmas 1964 was a day I would never forget. I was 12 years old, my sister was 10, and our lives were utterly transformed that day — a day traumatic and ultimately formative.

It wasn't Santa Claus who came that Christmas to our modest apartment over a bottle warehouse in Manzanillo. It was the cadre, the bearded troopers, the milicianos, the enablers of Fidel Castro, who had seized power in Cuba almost six years earlier.

My dad was not a politician. After years of hard work, he owned his business, and he loved his family and freedom. One day, they came to his shop and they said, "Mario Antonio Fernandez, give us your keys. You will now work for the government." He

"Papi's on the front left (alongside his employees) in El Polar, my father's first business in Manzanillo. Eventually he added a bar. I can remember him arguing with his ham supplier, saying he was overbilling. He then started preparing his own hams and supplying other enterprises."

I will do this and I will finish it. And, somehow, it will give greater meaning to my life and to the things I hold most dear.

"I was so tired that I truly envied that resting colt."

gave them the keys. He had no choice, but he said, "I will not work for you." That was his choice.

Shortly thereafter, he also asked for a visa to leave the country. He was not alone. It was a couple of years earlier that the government started to confiscate private businesses, large or small. Along with the others who had asked to leave the country, we now were called by many gusanos (worms). We were "worms" until the day we left.

Those in charge did not welcome opposition or dissent. Some people, in fact, were executed to dramatize the consequences of opposing the new system. More than a million people left the country (about 15 percent of the population) during the next few years. We were not alone.

Moreover, my father had made some inconvenient and powerful enemies. When they took his business away, they said it was because he allowed prostitution in one of the sandwich shops. Of course, that was nonsense. It wasn't even physically possible, given

"I WAS CLOSER TO THE STARS THAN EVER BEFORE . . . GETTING CLOSER TO A GOAL, WITHOUT KNOWING WHAT IT WAS."

the shop's size, and no one in the whole town truly believed the outrageous allegation.

Even though he knew an appeal would be futile, he went through the process. Three of the five people on the appeals board, known as a "people's tribunal," were his customers. Now, they were the all-powerful, with elevated status in the new order.

He stood before this appeals board and told the members, "I concur with you that there are a lot of whores in the world and a few in this town, and here are the names of three in this town." Then, he took out the receipts of the three people on the tribunal who owed him money. That shows you the kind of backbone he had — and still has.

As for my mother, Lieba Fernandez Gomez, I remember that during the revolution, there was a skirmish in our town between the Batista and Castro forces. The roof of my house was where the Castro guerillas staged their assault on the Batista soldiers who took refuge in a nearby theater. I remember my mother taking my sister, Pili, and me, pushing us to the floor, putting a sofa over us and covering us with her body, because bullets were coming over the balcony wall. That tells you a lot of what you need to know about my mother.

That's the kind of courage both my mother and father showed, and after Castro took over, my parents said, "We're not sending you to school to be brainwashed by these Communists." For the next three or four years, I did not go to school. One of the women who lived down the street was a teacher. Her children (Graciela and Luis Francisco Soto) became our best friends. That lady used to come to our house and give me and Pili classes on everything that we were missing in school.

So, on that Christmas Day of 1964, we were, to put it mildly, invited to leave Cuba. A military truck drove up, and my parents and sister and I were hustled into it. I was in my pajamas. We went to a field. A DC-3 landed. They put us on it. The plane could hold about 20 passengers, and two other families were aboard. We later learned that it was not unusual for Castro's thugs to rid themselves of dissidents in this way. Others had preceded us; and others would follow.

Tens of thousands of others were less fortunate in their attempts to escape oppression and abuse by the new regime in their homeland. I remember one person in particular. He left before we did. He was a few years older than I — taller, a handsome and friendly teenage son of my English teacher, Joaquin Muñiz. Only God knows what happened to his soul and to the souls of so many others who took to the sea. It was a treacherous trip and, in the majority of cases, those who embarked on it, in small boats or homemade rafts, were doomed to fail.

As I grew older, there would be many times — far too many times — that I would read about or hear about another group of brave, desperate Cubans who were lost at sea. Yet, each time, I thought back to my childhood and to the young man who never was to be seen again. I remember the anguish in my teacher's eyes as the days passed and news failed to arrive that his son had made it out. Anguish turned to tears, and the man aged in front of my eyes.

Fortunately, I eventually heard that my teacher, Mr. Muñiz, finally made it to the U.S. and that two of his other sons live here.

For me, that Christmas Day trip was not a bad experience; it was more like a sad adventure. After all, as the plane flew into the night, I was closer to the stars than ever before. I felt as if I were getting closer to a goal, without knowing what it was. But, at some point during that flight, I became frightened and held my sister's hand. Where are we going? Why did they do this to my family? Then, the ultimate wake-up call:

Why do my parents look so tense? Why are my father's eyes so red and why is he rarely blinking? They were afraid for us and themselves.

It was a long flight.

Basically, we were kicked out because my father had asked for that visa and had made those enemies. We had no visa, we had no passports, but they kicked us out anyway. At the time, the Cuban system was like a pressure cooker. The government wanted to relieve the pressure, so it got people like us out. It killed others.

When the government officials said go, it was go. We left everything behind. Like the Jews did before, during and after the Holocaust and at so many other times in their history, and like many, many other Cubans did. We're not unique. I never forget that my story is one among millions of such stories.

The Man at the Fence

We had no idea where we were going. Imagine the terror. My dad was 36 years old, my mother younger. They were responsible for our family. Imagine the terror in their mind.

So, the airplane landed and I remember that the weather when we left Cuba was humid and warm, and now we landed in a place where the weather seemed very cold. We had no coats. We had no money. We had no ID. We had no idea where we were.

It turned out to be Mexico City, where we were processed in a small cabin, far from the commercial air terminal. Close to that cabin was a chain-link fence — and, on the other side, a man with his hands on the fence was watching everything. After the Mexicans processed us, they said, "Go outside and see the guy who's over there." This man, Eugenio, was a Cuban who had been in our shoes a few months earlier. He made it his duty to come to the airport every night, and he made it a point to see if he could help anyone who was arriving, as he had arrived so recently.

Eugenio took us to a convent, where nuns put us up for that night. Before long, they placed us and a few others with Mexican families that kept us and fed us and gave us clothing. Next we stayed in a small motel, full of other Cubans. Once a week, to help us out, the nuns would send a box of powdered milk and cheese and things like that from the convent.

The man at the fence and my father became friends. One day, Eugenio asked my father, "Do you want to go with me to the airport at night?" My father was not allowed to work in Mexico, so he would go with Eugenio every night and stand by the fence. Every night. Once or twice a week, a flight would come in, and they would try to help whoever came off that flight by taking them by bus to the convent.

And one day — remember, I was only 12 — my father said, "Hey, Eugenio got his visa to leave for the U.S. You will come to the fence with me tonight." I went to the airport. It was one of Eugenio's last nights there. He looked right at me and he said, "You have one job. Your job is to make sure that everybody who comes through here is better off because they met you."

It didn't hit me until years later: "You have to take care of those who come after you."

I never saw Eugenio again.

Like all of us, I can point to many special moments in life, moments that sculpt us into the men or women we are, moments that become part of us. I can point to four or five particularly telling moments. That was one of them. "You have to take care of those who come after you."

That forms one of the core values of my life. It informs how I relate to my family and to my friends and associates and to the people whose paths I cross. At the very center of my soul, I hope and pray that my children and grandchildren — that all of our children and grandchildren — take this to heart and act on it whenever they have an opportunity.

Remember: You have to take care of those who come after you.

SEPTEMBER 22

Saint-Jean-Pied-de-Port And so it begins, under a clear sky and with a cool breeze

Cesar and I began today, heading up the road. We crossed a small wooden bridge and left Saint-Jean-Pied-de-Port and its beautiful view what seems like hours ago. Come on, Cesar, off we go! On behalf of children in need everywhere! We're doing this for you guys.

As we climbed above the town and reached the crest of the first of many mountains we saw on this day, we looked back. It was wonderful. On departure, the fog was heavy and one could barely see 100 yards away, but now we were above the fog, the clouds. The town couldn't be seen, but the top of the hills around us stood out as islands surrounded by a puffy sea of white. It was like looking at a white, calm ocean, with only the color blue missing.

We walked through open meadows and forests so thick it was like moving through a tunnel. We crossed the border between France and Spain. It was barely noticeable. Then, the downhill, by far the roughest part of the day. Dead tired, we arrived in late afternoon in the small Spanish village of Roncesvalles. We are hungry, dirty and in need of a fresh bed, any bed. There is great history here, where the French fought the Basques after sacking Pamplona.

Tomorrow morning, we will discover the hardest part of each day . . . to get moving again.

"In Saint-Jean-Pied-de-Port, France, on the evening before our first day on the trail, I didn't want to get lost as we headed out of town. So I walked alone to the outskirts of town. By accident I snapped this picture as I tried to set up the camera."

"High in the Pyrenees, only the whistle of the wind and the bells on the sheep could be heard."

SEPTEMBER 23

Village of Burguete

We came out of the trail and I was looking for a bathroom. The first person I asked responded without hesitation: "Come in, peregrino!" Everyone you meet says "Buen camino!" *Good road*, which in this context really means *have a safe pilgrimage*. How can you not love this place, these people, this adventure?

SEPTEMBER 24

High in the mountains near Akerreta

The sky is so gorgeous, the mountains so serene. I reach up and around. I can touch angels — angels who are going to do good.

We arrived at our lodge, and it was wonderful. Small, but well-appointed, with soft comfortable chairs, a small seating area full of books, overlooking the mountains.

CHAPTER **TWO**

A NEW LAND; A NEW LIFE

"Seeking the greater good . . . to enhance the quality of people's lives, particularly among God's poor, oppressed and neglected."

About six months after arriving in Mexico, we received our U.S. visas and we made it to New York City, where I spent my teenage years. We're talking about a five-story tenement at Broadway and West 136th Street. It's a pretty nice neighborhood now, but back then, on my doorstep, guys were shooting up with heroin.

Back in Manzanillo, we lived in an apartment on the second floor of a very modest building. The window of my bedroom did not have glass, only a wood shutter that sloped downward to block the rain. My grandfather lived out in the country, in a small house surrounded by fields.

Remember: My dad was a sandwich shop owner. He was not an industrialist. He did not own casinos. He did not own sugar mills. We came from a humble background. We lived in a rental unit above a bottle warehouse. As you can imagine, it was not a rich neighborhood. There was not a single traffic light in our town. To go from there to New York was a culture shock. To see the crime, the drug use, the urinating against the buildings.

Time went by and I was in a public junior high school and, to be honest, I did not fit in. I was always a little anti-authoritarian, and I was still learning English and dealing with the culture shock and . . . I didn't fit in. But I needed to be acknowledged, so I was in a difficult way. Soon, we moved farther north in Manhattan, to an apartment near the George Washington Bridge, and I transferred to a small parochial school — Saint Rose of Lima School.

"The scene near my grandfather's home." At right is the top floor of the rental apartment *"through which bullets came flying."*

A new school year began as I entered eighth grade. The school bell rang. All the students lined up for their designated classes when Julian, just ahead of me in line, turned around and said, "Are you new? Stay away from Rodney because he will beat up all the new kids." It was not my day. I sat in my seat and, before long, I felt a sting on my neck. With my left hand I reached back and picked up a spitball, still stuck to my bare neck. As I turned around, the boy right behind me took another shot . . . another spitball, this time on my face.

In my broken, barely comprehensible English, I told him, "Don't do that." He ignored me and did it again and grinned. I waited until the lunch break and I sought him out in the playground. He was a few inches taller than I was, but I knew what I had to do. Even if I lost, I had to confront him, so I grabbed him by his jacket and challenged him. "Want to fight?"

"My father and me outside our apartment in New York City and, at right, the same location with my son Cristofer and me."

Now, I was in too far to back down. He began to take off his jacket. Other kids circled around us and someone yelled, "Fight! Fight!" Rodney was going to kick my butt and I knew it, so I had to get one shot in. Boom! Without warning, I hit him as hard as I could, hard enough for him to fall down, but he was up in a second and proceeded to give me a good beating.

He won. Just as I expected, he kicked my butt. But there was a silver lining. The next day, as he walked toward me before school, I was ready for another fight, but he didn't swing at me. He said, "I'm Rodney," and put his hand on my shoulder.

This would not be the last time I saw Rodney. Not long after, he actually rose to my defense and protected me from another beating, this time on a subway train. Oddly, I stumbled on him much later, during my years in the U.S. Army. When you meet someone, you just never know what's in store down the road for both of you.

Xavier High School: Sacrifice and Deferred Gratification

Some time after my first encounter with Rodney, I was riding the subway and saw this kid wearing a military uniform. He carried himself with distinction. Something just clicked inside me and I approached him and he told me, no, he wasn't in the military. He said he was in high school at a place called Xavier. It's a Jesuit school right in the heart of Manhattan that has been educating kids since 1847.

I went to my teacher and said, "This is the school I want to go to — Xavier High School." She said, "Are you kidding? That's one of the top schools in the city. It's difficult to get in there."

But I managed it. I went there and spoke with them and one thing led to another, and I was one of three people who received scholarships that year.

I was very proud and I told my father that I received a scholarship and he asked, "Because of your grades?" And I said, "No, because I'm a minority." He gave me that "look" that parents can give and he said, "Stand up. Tell me, how does that work?" I said, "I received a scholarship because I'm a minority." He said, "No. You don't take charity. You have two arms and two legs. You get a job. You pay half the tuition and I pay half the tuition."

To cover my half of the tuition, I worked from my freshman through senior years at the New York State Psychiatric Institute, part of Presbyterian Hospital, in Manhattan, 6 to 9 p.m. every weekday. My job? Cleaning the cages that held animals used in experiments. I also fed them and mopped the floors. On weekends, I worked at the American Museum of Natural History, in the kiosk beside the entrance to the subway station. I sold plastic dinosaurs, key chains and things like that. Not glorious or lovely, but I paid half my tuition in high school.

And that was the second of those special moments and special lessons, and it came from my parents.

I learned about sacrifice and deferred gratification. Nothing that comes easily is worth learning. If it comes hard, it becomes a lesson. If it is hard, if it causes you to sweat, to think, to fall and get up . . . that's the learning experience. If it comes easily, you forget about it in a second. My learning came from sacrifice.

"I COULDN'T TAKE MY EYES OFF THE OTHER PATRONS, THE TOP LAYER OF NEW YORK SOCIETY."

Xavier turned out to be a transformative experience for me. The emphasis at this elite school was on scholarship and character development, and we had opportunities that I otherwise never could have imagined. For instance, one teacher occasionally took a few of us to hear the New York Philharmonic.

The objective, of course, was to develop an appreciation for fine music, but I took away another lesson. I couldn't take my eyes off the other patrons, the top layer of New York society. I watched how they spoke so softly to each other; how economical their movements were; how controlled and refined they seemed. I harkened back to those early days, when I was looking at — and reaching for — the stars I used to see while lying on the roof of my apartment building in Cuba.

I thought: I am getting closer. I thought: This is how successful Americans behave. I thought: This is what I will become.

Talking with Father Vincent Duminuco

At the same time, however, back there at Xavier, I still was a little noncompliant, a little rebellious, at best a C student. More than once, I was invited to apply someplace else, another school, but I hung in there. Finally, the principal of Xavier caught up to

"Second only to my parents, Father Duminuco became the most important mentor of my life. In 2015, a ceremony will take place adjacent to Xavier High in New York City where ground will be broken on the school's first new building in a half-century — the Duminuco-Fernandez Building."

me and he said, "Look, after 3 o'clock, you come to my office." Now, any kid who's told to come to the principal's office, he figures he's in trouble.

His name was Father Vincent Duminuco. From that afternoon onward, he talked to me every day, but never about school subjects. He didn't talk to me about math. He didn't talk to me about science. He didn't talk to me about geography. He talked to me about ethics, values, sacrifice, leaving the world a better place than you found it. He talked to me about living an ethical life, living a life of honor, protecting your reputation. We talked like this almost every day. Not about school subjects, but about life, about being a man. That turned out to be an enduring contribution to the man I became.

This is what Father Duminuco once wrote:

"Education in Jesuit schools seeks to transform how youth look at themselves and other human beings, at social systems and societal structures, at the global community of humankind and the whole of natural creation. If truly successful, Jesuit education results ultimately in a radical transformation not only of the way in which people habitually think and act, but of the very way in which they live in the world, men and women of competence, conscience and compassion, seeking the greater good in terms of what can be done out of a faith commitment with justice to enhance the quality of people's lives, particularly among God's poor, oppressed and neglected."

Let me repeat: "To enhance the quality of people's lives, particularly among God's poor, oppressed and neglected."

Next to the values that I learned from my parents, the most important person during my early years was that priest, Father Duminuco. For four years, he focused on me, making me what I am today. Little did I know then that, decades later, the good Father would resurface in my life.

Learning by Observation

Education can take many forms. Book learning? Sure. Many of my most meaningful and personally gratifying

Leaving Xavier after class, and felt happy. But in an hour I would change and clean cages and sweep floors.

Chapter 2

Castros: of Celtic origin, referring to a fortified settlement in pre-Roman times. "That pile of rocks is all that's left of this castro!"

Sacrifice. Perseverance. Good humor. These are key qualities, and I am fortunate to have had an opportunity to acquire them.

good works have involved significant contributions to educational institutions.

But the lessons we absorb from our teachers and our parents by listening to their advice and watching them steer their lives, that, too, is a form of education. For instance, I learned to keep my priorities in order, to manage my time effectively, to wake up earlier and work harder than the next person, to remain focused, to practice integrity in business and compassion in all elements of life.

I learned all this, and more, simply by observing those around me and opening myself to the examples they set. This has worked for me. It can work for anyone.

So, I graduated from Xavier High School in December 1971 and, just a month later, I began taking classes at the University of New Mexico, in Albuquerque, though not for long. I had thought I wanted to be an architect, but it was not a good fit.

A month into school, the dean of the School of Architecture and Planning addressed the students and, on that day, my life changed. He said: "If you want to study architecture and hope to be rich one day, you will be disappointed." About

"I WALKED OUT OF THE UNIVERSITY. I NEVER EVEN FINISHED THE LECTURE ... I WAS DONE WITH ARCHITECTURE."

10 minutes later, I walked out of the university. I never even finished the lecture. I listened to what he said, I absorbed the lesson he was sharing, and I was educated, though not in the way he intended. Bottom line, I was done with architecture.

Though I wasn't at the University of New Mexico long, I do recall an event that even now makes me smile.

I had been attending classes for only a few days when a fellow student approached me as I walked across campus. He also was a freshman, and his family lived in New Mexico. In a very polite manner, typical of those born in the Southwest, he said he had noticed my accent. I told him that I had arrived in New Mexico only a few weeks earlier from New York City, but I had been born in Cuba.

A big smile came across his face. "I remember Cuba as a kid," he said. "My parents used to drive us there once in a while to buy bread and it was always warm." Huh?

Driving to Cuba to buy bread? That stopped me right in my tracks. "Yes," he said, "the drive on the weekend was something we looked forward to, and I still remember the smell of the bread inside the car."

Now, I was really confused. "What are you talking about?" I asked with a smile. I figured he was pulling some sort of joke on me. Now, the roles had changed as he looked at me with confusion.

He said: "Yes, Cuba! The Navajo reservation north of the city." It turns out that there is a tiny town called Cuba, New Mexico, and it's adjacent to that reservation. I laughed, and we continued along our path across campus.

A Gift From an Unlikely, and Terrifying, Source

With the draft looming over me, I enlisted in the U.S. Army in 1972, accepted a challenge, and found myself in the Army's 82nd Airborne Division, a unit that, as you would guess, jumps out of airplanes.

It wasn't an easy duty, but the tests I passed and the rigors I endured during training fortified my body and my will.

On June 30, 1972, I wrote this in a letter home to my parents, in my still-broken English:

"Every day, we have to run 5 miles before breakfast to get to where we shoot the rifles, and that kills us. At first, I would fall behind, but not anymore. I am getting in great shape, with many muscles. On Thursday, we had to go to the 'school of prisoners of war,' where they gave us an idea of what can happen if one is captured. When we got there, they took our shoes and socks. Then, we had to walk about half a mile over small rocks. After that, they put us in a small room where we had to walk hunched over, and the food we had to eat was rice, water and raw chicken. And, if we didn't eat it all, they would beat us up. (The food was exquisite.)"

Sacrifice. Perseverance. Good humor. These are key qualities, and I am fortunate to have had an opportunity to acquire them. Also curiosity and . . . certainly not insubordination, but let's call it . . . audacity and inquisitiveness. Though no discipline issues ever were involved, I was honorably discharged in 1975 at the same rank I held when I took the oath. I had been promoted twice and demoted twice, essentially for asking "Why?" too many times.

Another key and influential moment in my life came during one of those Airborne training missions. I was 19 years old. That day not only changed my life; it turbocharged my life.

As was the case during most days in the Army, we awoke at 5:30 a.m., endured an early 5-mile run and went to a staging area to wait for the order to get in the planes. I was one of 19 soldiers to walk into the belly of that C-130 aircraft. Engines on. Climb to 1,250 feet. Stand up and hook up the parachute line. Check your buddy's gear, and he checks your gear.

The light in the back and front of the plane turns from red to green. Now, you're going to jump this day. One by one, each soldier steps into the sky. So far, so good.

Then, my gift arrives, though it certainly doesn't seem that way at first.

My parachute only partially deploys. At 1,250 feet, there is very little time to react. My reaction is automatic — because of the training I received. As the ground rushes closer, I work at popping out my reserve chute.

It finally opens when I am maybe 300 feet off the ground. That's good, but not really ideal. I land hard, and suffer hairline fractures to both ankles, but I walk away.

On that day I received one of the most important gifts in my lifetime, but I did not recognize it until a few years later. I could have died. It was my first real awareness that my days would be numbered. We are all "terminal," but I learned that as a very young man.

This gift made me appreciate life more than most people do, particularly at that tender age. It made me live each day with one persistent thought in mind: I would pretend that I would live only for another week — just one more week.

This attitude made me exceedingly productive — and, I'm told, determined and imbued with a certain, shall we say, intensity. I was not scared or upset when I had my first heart attack at 51 — nor when I had a second one at 54, and not when I received a diagnosis of prostate cancer at 59.

Each time, I was reminded that we are all on God's timetable, and it's up to us to make a difference. You have to live your life as though you're going to die on Monday. My kids say that's morbid. I say it's life.

All it takes is one more moment before you plummet into the ground, one more step before you hit that land mine, and you don't know when it will be. So, as this plays out in, say, business, if it takes my competitors a year to do something, it should take me 90 days. That's how I work. That's how I live, at least up to now.

Let me tell you something else: You must have passion. Find your passion, and dedicate yourself to it.

Cuando llegamos alli, nos quitaron los zapatos y los medias. Entonces tuvimos que caminar como por ½ milla en pudicitos chiquitos. Después nos pusieron en un cuartico en cual teníamos que estar probados y la comida que tuvimos que comer fue arroz, aguay y carne de pollo (cruda). Y si no lo comíamos todo nos daban una entrada a pinazos (la comida estaba esquisita).

Bueno escribanle __ los dulces. y los fotos

De su hijo que no los olvida y los quiere.

Miguel Benito fernandez

"MAD CUBAN"

This is a
C-130 just like
the ones I
used to have
to jump out of.

"This letter was kept for more than 40 years by my parents. It was written in the latter half of 1972."

SEPTEMBER 25

Between Akerreta and Pamplona

As I woke up in the morning, I stretched out, and walked outside. I sat on the ground, a 4-foot wall behind me. It was but a few minutes before I felt something touching my hair and then landing on my shoulder. It was a white kitten. I began talking to it, while hoping that no one was watching or listening.

Cesar and I joined four other people for breakfast. "No eggs," the innkeeper said. "Eat lots of bread, homemade jams and drink coffee or café con leche." Someone asked, "No eggs?" The innkeeper responded, "You can if you like, but you may not be wanting a stomachache on the trail." Wise advice. I followed that simple rule for the next 40 days.

Today was very hot as we came off the mountains. The trail followed a river for most of the day, and we saw old guys fly-fishing for trout.

These last four days of hiking have been both wonderful and grueling. The first day, although it's the most physically challenging, was the easiest, as the body was rested. From the second day on, I have begun to recognize that I am not as young as I used to be. It is a grind. The weather is beautiful, as God has blessed us with incredibly clear skies and temperatures that vary between the low 70s and low 50s. Climbing and descending the Pyrenees has produced myriad colors and sounds, high mountain meadows and deep forests covered with moss. On Day One, we actually saw no one. Since then, our encounters with other pilgrims and locals have been sparse and no more than half a dozen a day.

Today, we begin to head down toward the warmer plains near Pamplona. The temperature will be much warmer (high 80s) and the low tonight will be in the 60s.

People are very friendly, and this journey truly is a delight, even with painful muscles. The worst so far has been the blisters for me (none for Cesar). I have developed four between my toes, and one is bleeding, though I have been treating them since they began to feel painful.

It's strange how the mind works. The first half of the day passes by quite quickly, but the second half comes to a crawl and it seems as though we are never going to get to our destination. Yet, what keeps us moving is the thought of the children who are so unfairly experiencing a much worse time and certainly have much more courage than we do. I hope all of you are well and all of the children in need are getting better.

It is really enjoyable to be walking with my old friend Cesar Alvarez. We have been together for so many years and now we have all the time in the world to recall once-lost memories. It is almost sinful to laugh as much as we do. I really hope that we get to do this again together some day or that he extends his stay with me.

Chapter 2

"As Cesar Alvarez and I walked into the small mountain village of Viscarett, we passed this abandoned church, originally built seven centuries ago. From this tower were witnessed builders, farmers and knights."

"To me, God is goodness. God is doing good to and for others."

SEPTEMBER 26

Still between Akerreta and Pamplona

We are on a light diet of ham and cheese on a baguette for dinner. That's about it. Oh, I forgot — and water. I am proud that Cesar is still with me during this first week, and then he will return. I will continue for the next four weeks alone.

It has taken us two days to cover this terrain — mountains, valleys and the most beautiful trail along a fast-flowing river. The sound of the river was refreshing. The water in the river was freezing, but good for angry feet! We are in the middle of God's country. There are church bells everywhere on the half-hour and on the hour, but in the countryside there also are cowbells! It's music to our ears.

The country begins to open up and we can see Pamplona in the distance, with its high, protective walls. I wonder, how many battles have been fought there? How many lives have been lost? We are now just outside the city walls. We enter via one of the old gates, walk down the narrow streets and ask for directions to our hotel. It is the same hotel at which Ernest Hemingway, Orson Welles and other notables have stayed. We were so tired that we took only a brief walk after a warm shower, and then straight back to bed. As we walked the hallway in the hotel, we could hear snoring from nearly every room. We are all in this together.

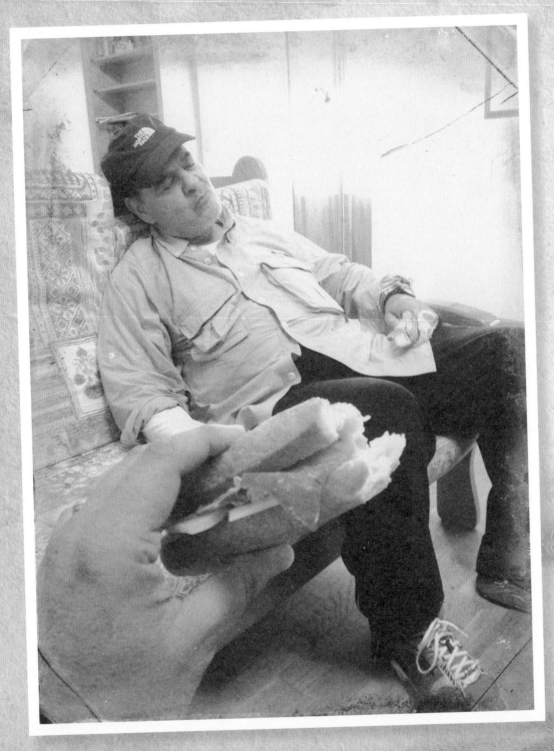

"Exhausted? You bet. We were three or four days into the trip. Here's my friend Cesar, both of us thankful that we kept half of our lunch in our backpacks."

CHAPTER **THREE**

I AM MY PARENTS' SON

"You must work hard while you are young — or you will have to work hard until the day you die."

My father (Papi to me) was wise beyond his years, and I can prove it by sharing with you one crucially important insight he shared with me when I was in my mid-teens.

At that age, I had my doubts, my insecurities, my temptations, just like any other young man looking toward the future. All of those nights and weekends at work, mopping floors at the hospital's animal laboratory, certainly didn't help.

I doubted the wisdom of my work — of any work. My friends from Xavier went out on weekends, attending family gatherings and picnics or the occasional party or prom. I knew I was missing out on the fullness of the high school experience that so many American teenagers enjoy.

I understood that I had to work, but the loss of those weekends hit me particularly hard, so I shared my frustration with my mom. She always has been my dad's most enthusiastic supporter. If there was any dissension, it was behind closed doors, and neither Pili nor I ever heard a word of it. She understood my feelings, and I knew that my comment would be passed on to my father.

Remember, my dad was a man who, to preserve his dignity and express his opposition to the overseers of the Castro government, forfeited all his business assets. Of primary importance to him was the future of his children. He knew that Pili and I would benefit from a better life away from the totalitarian regime.

He was a man without the benefits of a formal education, a man who created his original business out of nothing. He arrived in these great United States of America in May 1965, not speaking or understanding a word of English.

But in this foreign land, within a week of our arrival, he landed a job, and then a second job.

"WE ALWAYS ARE SURROUNDED BY OPPORTUNITIES, BUT IT REQUIRES EFFORT TO SEE THEM AND ACT UPON THEM."

Except for that one moment on the plane when we left Cuba, I never saw a hint of doubt or fear in his eyes. When it came to providing for his family, there was not a job that was beneath him. Within a few days of starting his job as a breakfast cook in downtown Manhattan, he secured a second job as a waiter and bartender at Kennedy International Airport in Queens, a long subway and bus ride away.

He never missed a beat! He set out to do again what he had done before, to provide for us as well as he could — to build a life for his family.

After he completed his 6 a.m. shift, making eggs, bacon and anything else ordered, he took the subway home, arriving around noon. A quick lunch, a brief nap and he was on the train again, heading to his second job. There, way out at the airport, he worked from 6 p.m. to midnight. Then, the long trip back home for a few hours of sleep before awakening, once again, at 5 a.m.

New York City in the early 1970s: "Papi and me at the dinner table."

Chapter 3

We all have made many mistakes. If not, then we have not tried hard enough to get out of our comfort zones.

**Puente la Reina (the Queen's Bridge), Spain,
"the place from where Cesar and I parted, and I
walked on alone."**

Soon, during one of his morning walks to the subway, my dad noticed an opportunity. (He frequently told me, "We always are surrounded by opportunities in life. But it requires effort to see them and act on them and benefit from them.") This opportunity was passed by thousands of people every day, yet only my dad recognized it and acted upon it. It was a clothing manufacturing business that happened to be owned by a Jewish man who, not so very long ago, also was a newly arrived refugee.

Remember, my dad had been in this new land for less than three weeks and he already had two jobs. But, when he was paid at the end of his third week, he had a plan. This time, instead of walking by the clothing manufacturer, he went inside. A middle-aged clerk soon realized that my dad did not speak English. Fortunately, the clerk spoke Spanish.

"HE ALWAYS PAID IN CASH, NEVER CREDIT, AND COULD NOT SPEAK ENGLISH, EXCEPT 'EXCUSE ME.'"

Dad said that he wanted to buy clothes and then resell them. The clerk responded that the business only sold to wholesale customers. Selling just a few pieces to my dad? Sorry, it could not be done.

Papi asked the clerk to introduce him to the manager or owner. Once again, the clerk tried to discourage him, saying that the owner did not speak Spanish. "That's okay," Papi said. "You will translate."

Now, here comes the owner's son. Again, my father is told that this is not possible — he cannot buy just a few pieces of clothing. But Papi had faced much bigger obstacles in his life, and this man was not about to dissuade him, so he tried many different approaches in response to many different objections.

During all of this, an old man was observing from nearby. Finally, he intervened. He was the owner, and he politely told my father that, indeed, the business only responded to large orders, but he did have returned leather coats that contained minor stitching flaws. He would sell these at a discount.

Unfortunately, my father had enough money for only two coats. Once again, the owner's son said that Dad needed to buy more. Once again, the father overruled his son and told my father, "I will sell you the two coats."

As time passed, my father was told that the owner sold him the coats because he had once been a refugee himself. So here we have an example of good deeds, paying it forward. An old refugee to America overrode the rules to help a new refugee to America, and his wife and children.

My father sold both coats by going door to door along our New York City block

"Before he got home for lunch, my father sold two leather coats door to door on our New York City block. He doubled his investment, and then went on to sell many more such coats."

before he got home for lunch. One was sold for cash; the other on credit — $10 down and $5 per week at a total price that represented a 100 percent profit.

The next day, Papi went back to the manufacturer and purchased three coats. Within a few months he was an established client and he never bought leather coats from anyone else. He always paid in cash, never credit, and could not speak English, except "Excuse me."

THE GIFT OF OUR FATHERS

We all have made many mistakes. If not, then we have not tried hard enough to get out of our comfort zones. But one of the worst mistakes I ever made was not completely recognizing my father for what he was and is. Many of us probably have made this mistake.

We think of our fathers as aging older men, but we forget that they are us. They once were newborns helpless at birth, just as we were. They once were young kids who learned to ride bicycles, just as we did. They once were teenagers, helpless and confused when first meeting girls they liked, just as we were. They once dealt with first jobs and wondered and worried about their futures, just as we did.

They had children and worried about them. They may have wished that they said "I love you" to their kids more often. They grew older without fully recognizing it.

And they protected their children. Where did you learn to protect and guide your children? You learned it from the person you called Papi, Dad, Daddy, Pop. Our fathers gave us a great gift, didn't they?

A year later, he was still buying and selling coats, and he expanded to jewelry by buying in New York's famed Diamond District, along West 47th Street between Fifth and Sixth avenues. Papi used the same door-to-door, cash-or-credit, foot-pounding technique that worked so nicely with the leather jackets. By 1969, he was making more than $100,000 per year when the average salary in the U.S. was $5,800 annually. And, now, he spoke and understood English quite a bit better.

In the years following our arrival in 1965, we moved twice, as we slowly became upwardly mobile. First, we moved to that northern Manhattan apartment near the

George Washington Bridge. Then, we moved even more to the north — to an apartment near Van Cortlandt Park in the Bronx.

This was very close to a more affluent neighborhood called Riverdale. Not quite there, but at least we could see the future if Dad — if all of us — kept working hard.

This brings us back to that important insight that my father shared with me and that I never forgot, and that I need to share with you.

One day, I complained to my father. "Why do you work so hard," I asked, "and never go to my school? We never seem to do anything together."

He thought for a moment, and this is what he said:

"You must work hard when you are young — or you will have to work hard until the day you die."

My father's gifts included a great blend of gentleness and toughness — much like Crusader, my first and my favorite Friesian.

SEPTEMBER 27

Pamplona to Puente la Reina

Another beautiful day. I am hoping the next month continues this way. The highlight between these two towns is a mountaintop called Alto de Perdón, "Height of Forgiveness." The distance between Pamplona and Puente la Reina is not long, but it is time-consuming. From the heights of the Alto de Perdón, one can almost see Pamplona to the east and Puente la Reina to the west, but the climb up and the walk down are treacherous. From this point, you not only enjoy a beautiful landscape but also windmills as far as the eye can see, all along the ridges. In addition, one sees sculptures of multiple characters representing the myriad pilgrims who have passed here.

"We were clearly pilgrims in the 'off-season.' There was little trace of the scent of humankind."

SEPTEMBER 28

Estella

El Camino to Estella is dotted with small towns and villages, and a landscape of wheat and barley fields and vineyards and olive groves. Estella is a graceful and compact town situated on both sides of the Rio Ega, and is best known for its vast numbers of Roman-era monuments.

A highlight is the 12th century Palacio de los Reyes de Navarra, featuring a work of art depicting the eighth-century duel between Roland, a Frankish military leader under Charlemagne, and the giant Ferragut.

I may be out of touch for the next day or so as the journey takes us through desolate but safe areas. During this first week of the walk, I have been to the snow-capped heights of the Pyrenees, through forest so dense that daylight turns to night, through open mountain meadows where all you hear is the whistling wind and the sheep's bells that you can almost never see. It feels mystical.

I have met a man who has been living in these mountains by his own means. It is such a peaceful place. He asked that we keep our voice volume low so as to not "disturb the land." We ate the freshest goat cheese and blueberry jam I have ever experienced, and tomatoes so sweet that I am sure a person with knowledge could squeeze sugar out of them.

Already, we've met a few people along the way, including three who have been friends for more than 30 years (ages 70, 66 and 64), who take the time to keep building their friendship. Cesar and I had dinner with them last night, and they were, to say the least, "colorful." They spoke about their decades-old relationship and how their friendship had survived marriages and time. Tonight would be their last night on El Camino, as they were off to Amsterdam to attend a concert.

What else?

- Walked over roads built by the Romans in 200 A.D.!
- Passed over bridges built in the 11th century.
- Got a little sick because of the heat and a little exhaustion, but I'll shake it off.
- Blisters continue to be a problem, primarily between the toes. I need to stop every few hours to adjust the dressings.
- As I head into Week Two, I feel emotionally charged. I think of the brave kids in need of care. And, yes, I admit that I am a little physically challenged at the moment.

Here's the big picture: I never had a bucket list, but if I were smart enough to have one, this journey would have been No. 1.

I am in love with the experience.

"The path between France and Roncesvalles, Spain, is called the 'Napoleon route,' which is the path Cesar Alvarez and I took. It was our first day of walking. The signs told us that it was just 2 hours and 15 minutes more to Roncesvalles. It took us five hours to arrive. We didn't rely on signs much anymore."

CHAPTER**FOUR**

LESSONS LEARNED, WISDOM RECEIVED

"Words worth following during my continuing journey through life"

As I began to grow and expand my horizons, I realized the wisdom of my father's words — words applicable not only to my work life, but also to life in general. A few years later, I was to find myself remembering those words as I started my first job after being honorably discharged from the U.S. Army.

During my time in the Army, my parents moved from New York City to Miami, the new home of so many displaced Cubans. Lacking a college degree but needing to work, my options were limited and, as I had learned in the Army, my personality was not conducive to being a good follower or employee.

So, I took a job that would allow me plenty of flexibility, if not much glamour: I became a door-to-door life insurance salesperson. In order to succeed, I needed to learn to accept rejection, as the vast majority of door knocks do not end with a sale.

I was one of many to be hired for a salary of $500 per month. For most, that was a pittance, but, for me, that was almost double what I made in the Army. I thought I had hit the lottery.

I understood the risk of receiving a token salary, but I focused on the potential rewards that came along with the deal — unlimited income potential in the form of commissions. Bottom line: The harder I worked, the more I could make.

I had never sold anything, except when I worked near the museum as a child. I hated the job, but loved the opportunity to prove myself.

Most of my coworkers would not last more than a few months. For them, it was feast or famine. When they had a good week, they would slack off for the next week or two. My approach was different — my goal was based on "consistency with persistency." I never relied on one big sale to help me reach the company's required monthly goal. Instead, I took the monthly goal and converted it to smaller weekly objectives.

I set out to hit or exceed the targets not by looking for "home runs" — that is, single large sales — but rather by connecting for multiple singles and doubles — smaller sales that would add up.

This required me to work longer and harder than my peers. When they were taking it easy during the weekend, I was still working — just as I had during my youth, just as my dad had taught me.

My efforts soon paid off, and I led the Florida region in sales. But I didn't like selling life insurance. Repeatedly sitting at a prospect's kitchen table, telling the family the importance of providing for survivors or covering the cost of a college education in case the head of the household lost his or her life was not pleasant. I simply did not like it.

B 33   BCT
3 RD PLATOON
FORT ORD
CALIFORNIA
9   JUNE 1972

*"Did I tell you that I was a little 'noncompliant'? Find the only soldier with sunglasses
(not permitted, of course). That's me at age 19."*

Selling life insurance was the most rewarding financial product that the company had, and commissions varied from 50 to 90 percent of the first annual premium. On the opposite side of the spectrum, commission income for selling health insurance was very low — about 5 or 10 percent, paid monthly. Most of my coworkers were not interested in that. It was there that I identified an opportunity. As my dad would say: "See the opportunity and act on it."

An Evolving Business Model

At first I approached the top agents and offered to promote health insurance to their clients and prospects, both individuals and companies, and split the commissions equally. All they had to do was introduce me to the client and I would do all the work by selling and servicing the health insurance policy.

This was a no-brainer for them, and they all agreed. I had been in the insurance business for about six months, and the way I saw the arrangement was that I now had

"IF YOU ARE GOING TO HAVE PARTNERS, MAKE CERTAIN THAT YOU CONTROL 51 PERCENT OF THE ENTERPRISE."

the top-selling agents serving as my "birddogs" for new clients. During the next six months, my business grew to the point that I had to hire and pay for an assistant to help me coordinate all the business I was reaping. I knew I was onto something that I could build.

Soon, I expanded my corps of "birddogs" from five to 30. Now, with a proven model, I hired two, three, four and then more assistants. I also took on two partners who were part of the top-selling group of agents. We chose to formalize the partnership by calling it Fergus St. George and Affiliates. (Fer = Fernandez, Gus = Gustavo, and St. George = a derivative of our third partner's last name.) Our business continued to grow, but so did some problems.

As the partnership's second year began, I realized that I was generating more than half of the sales, but we were splitting the income in three equal parts. I did not think that was fair to me. I approached my two partners and told them that each would get only what he was responsible for generating and closing. Obviously, this new arrangement would work better for me, but worse for them. The partnership was dissolved.

Lesson learned: If you are going to have partners, make certain that you control 51 percent of the enterprise.

A year later, my revenue substantially increased and, in less than five years, my income also had grown from the four-figure range to six figures. I was now closer to being what my father excelled at — a good provider for my family.

Being a good provider also was evident in other ways. By doing well in my life, I was able to provide assistance to others whom I'd met on my journeys, individuals who briefly entered and left my life, giving me small windows of time in which to provide assistance.

The teachings I learned from the man at the fence in Mexico and from Father Dominuco at Xavier, and the work ethic and vision that my father bestowed upon me have allowed me to "take care of those who came after" me. It was now clearer than ever that those were words worth following during my continuing journey through life.

Chapter 4

Unfortunately, now I can feel the weather beginning to change. Summer is transitioning to winter.

Northern Spain's Meseta (plateau or 'table land'): "It's a lonesome and shadeless four-day hike on El Camino. I remember someone saying: "You can go crazy as you go dry.'"

OCTOBER 1
Torres del Rio, after a day of rest

I feel rejuvenated. Excited. Full of enthusiasm. Except for the two blisters that just won't go away. I have tried blister medications, compresses, creams, cold water and salt, whatever, but my "blister buddies" are still here, so as to remind me, "This is not just a walk!"

Well, it's 6:50 a.m., and I am out the door. A short 13 miles today, so it's not a long day. I will miss my dear friend Cesar Alvarez, who has been my companion and partner for the last week but now has returned home. We laughed and told stories, but today I will focus on a child at a hospital, and all I see will be through her eyes. All I experience will be for her benefit. The next four weeks I will walk alone. Buen camino, my friends!

Later in the day:
This has been an unusually hot day. As I hiked through a tiny village, I spotted a low stone fence around a two-story stone and mortar house — a fence that created a bit of shade. I took off my backpack and, as the sun edged closer and closer, I lay down and rested in that narrow strip of shade.

A window opened up on the second story of the house, and an old man poked his head out. He had to be in his 90s. My first thought as a paranoid American was, I'm trespassing. But he looked down and he said, "Buenos días, peregrino." Good morning, pilgrim. I told him I was leaving, but he said, "No. Rest."

So he closed his little window and, a few minutes later, as I was still there, the window opened up again and the old man said: "Peregrino!" I looked up, and he lowered a bottle of water and a banana on a string. I said, "Muchas gracias," and he responded in Spanish, "If I were younger, I would bring it down to you, but I'm too old to walk."

How can you not love an experience like that? How can you not love your fellow human beings?

Even later in the day:
I passed by the village of Ayegui, where I saw the well-known Fuente del Vino, the "Fountain of Wine," a tap of free wine provided by Bodegas Irache to fortify thirsty pilgrims on their way to Santiago. I was glad to see that there also was a water fountain, which was very welcome to me.

Unfortunately, now I can feel the weather beginning to change. Summer is transitioning into winter. Mist, rain and wind will come to be my constant companions.

OCTOBER 2

Nájera

Moving across the undulating terrain, I left behind the "autonomous community" of Navarra and entered La Rioja, both an autonomous community and a Spanish province. I passed through Viana, an attractive town circled by high walls and boasting stone mansions, many decorated with family crests. I entered Logroño, a city of rich tradition, but the cobblestone streets seemed drab and I found few people on the road. The city has changed little since the Middle Ages. I stopped in the historic quarter and sampled the local tapas.

Hoping to leave the rain behind me, I kept moving toward Nájera.

After about 8 miles, I passed Navarrete, a town of only about 2,600 residents, built during the 12th century. I continued my walk, surrounded by gentle terrain. This region is dominated by vineyards, and one of the more memorable moments came as I picked grapes that had fallen from the vines and enjoyed them under the protection of a large tree.

I am soaked and I am cold. Who could have said a week ago that this would be an experience worth remembering? But it is. Trust me, it is.

"Winter is close by. The wheat has been harvested, and there is no one in sight. I am alone, but I am not lonely."

CHAPTER **FIVE**

THE GIFT OF GRATITUDE, THE GIFT OF GIVING

"This is how I repay some of the debt I am feeling. You have to do what you can do."

My passions are these: My family — wife Constance, daughter Michelle and sons George, Alex, Michael and Cristofer, grandchildren Stella and Daniella, my parents, my sister, and all the others — and my friends; my work and my efforts to "take care of those who come after" me.

My family comes first, as it should, though I'll acknowledge that it might not always have seemed so. I burned through two previous marriages, largely because I devoted so much time and energy — so much of myself — to work. I think I have learned from those experiences; I certainly hope that I have.

Now, my wife, Constance, is my rock. We met when my partners and I were selling a business and she was a director of the company that was buying the business from

Back home: "My daughter Michelle took this picture as I fell asleep on a hammock. As always, Constance was there to catch me."

us. I remember the group coming into a restaurant and, as she passed by, she took my breath away. If ever there was love at first sight, this was it. A completely wonderful, giving, sensitive human being, Constance keeps me grounded, keeps me reminded about what truly is important in life.

I have one child with Constance, four other children and two granddaughters. I love them all, though of course, as in any family, we sometimes have our differences. If I have made any mistakes in raising them, I regret those mistakes — and I devote myself every day to learning from them and making up for them.

The way I see it, my job is not to make my children rich. My job is to provide some sort of safety net for them and to motivate them to live well. Put another way, ultimately, my job is to ensure their safety.

A long time ago, as my success in business began to hit critical mass, my father told me that my children should not know how prosperous we were becoming. I agreed with him, but I was perplexed. I asked him and, in truth, I asked myself, "How can I hide it?"

"SO, IT SEEMED TO ME THAT THE BEST APPROACH WAS TO TEACH THEM HOW TO MANAGE THEIR GROWING RESOURCES."

Let me say this: They are not spoiled rich kids. Through the years, each had been given a modest allowance to offset routine expenses. As they reached maturity, they also received rewards for getting good grades during their senior years in high school. They have been reprimanded if they crossed the line of politeness when interacting with people who work with us at home and in the office.

So, it seemed to me that the best approach was to teach them how to manage their growing resources. Starting at an early age, the children were required to attend meetings with attorneys and wealth managers. They also were — and are — expected to work, and not for me.

All five of my children serve as "owners" of our businesses through a family trust, but only one — my oldest, George — actually works for one of our companies. He

Chapters

"Remember what was done for you. It will be your turn one day to do this for some-body else."

"A view from my window outside Azpeitia in the Basque region of Spain. I came here to the Sanctuary of Loyola, the birthplace of the Jesuit order. After Father Duminuco's death, I returned a crucifix he had given me to his Jesuit home."

reports to a supervisor, he works in a cubicle rather than an office, and, I am pleased to report, I've been told he never, even remotely, has implied to others that he is an owner of the company.

The Rewards of Helping Others

My other passions — work and helping those in need — are so tightly intertwined that I don't know if they can be untangled, but let me try. First, let's discuss why and how I help others, and what I derive from it.

When I was in the Army, my salary was $287 a month. By the time I was discharged in 1975, my parents had moved from New York to Miami, so I moved to Miami, and I found that job selling insurance. I was new in town. Consequently, I had to go knock on doors.

This was hard work. You have to have thick skin. You have to be able to accept "no" 100 times for every "yes." My salary was about $500 a month.

I remember reading an article in the Miami Herald — this was in 1977 — about low-income neighborhoods in Rio de Janeiro. The people there were so impoverished that they had to connect illegally to gas lines. Many fires broke out and many children were hurt by those fires.

Here I am. I'm 24 years old. I'm making $500 a month, and what the guy at the fence in Mexico said kicks in, and what Father Duminuco said kicks in. To enhance the quality of people's lives, particularly among God's poor, oppressed and neglected.

So, I heard about a Brazilian teenager who, when she was a little baby in a crib, had lost her legs in a fire.

I saved and scrounged some money. I managed to bring this girl and her mother and father to Miami. I found them an apartment and I bought her a set of used prosthetics, and she was trained to use them to walk.

At my income level, I could not afford to spend much. But, for some reason, I took on this cause, and this 14-year-old girl received her prosthetic legs and was able to stand for the first time in her life.

That, right there, was my first conscious act of paying back. Believe me, it was not a question of having money, because I didn't have any money. It was because I felt I had to do something to help someone in that terrible situation. By the way, until this past year, I have never told anyone outside my very tight circle about that act.

What I learned from that random act of helping a stranger was that, yes, she

My whole life seemingly has been in fundraising, meaning I've met a lot of good people. None ranks higher with me than Mike Fernandez. He's a wonderful example of a charming, truly generous philanthropist. He's also challenging, dynamic, frustrating and, overall, delightful.

When Mike came on the board of the Miami Children's Health Foundation, I was struck by his charm — everyone is — but, more than that, I was impressed by his interest in patients. From there, a deeper friendship developed. Years later, over breakfast, Mike asked for a status report about the hospital and how he might help us. "We need a new emergency room," I said, "and we have a goal of $15 million to make it happen." He didn't hesitate. "Would $5 million help?" I was stunned, having given him no details or anything in the way of an in-depth understanding of the project. I drove back to the office in a daze.

When it came to naming the new trauma department, Mike wanted his family rather than himself to be recognized for this gift. Who knew that his granddaughter, Daniella, soon would need lifesaving heart surgery?

How many children has Mike helped? Who could know? But it's crystal clear that his philanthropy will benefit generations of children to come.

I cherish my friendship with Mike, and always will.

Ann E. Lyons

VICE PRESIDENT OF LEADERSHIP GIFTS
MIAMI CHILDREN'S HEALTH FOUNDATION

received a gift from a person she never met. But I was the person who felt the euphoria of happiness when I was told, "Mike, she is standing."

Priorities and Responsibilities

Since that day in 1977, I have become more involved in helping those in need, especially when it comes to children. In many cases, I did it with the participation of a special woman, Ann Lyons, vice president of programs and leadership gifts at a children's hospital, who never disappointed me, the patient's family or the patient.

The effort to help children is not over. It can never be over.

How can any of us put a price on a child's life? How do you put a price on a parent's face knowing his or her child is being taken care of? You can't put a price on it. All you can do is . . . all you can do to help.

As the years passed, I became more productive and, consequently, more successful. As I've said, I work hard to earn it, but I also work hard to make certain that it is

---

"HOW CAN I ACHIEVE WHAT I WAS MEANT TO ACHIEVE WHEN IT COMES TO HELPING OTHERS?"

---

properly used. First and foremost, I must make certain that my loved ones — my parents, wife, children, grandchildren and a few others — are financially secure. That is my first priority. Close behind that, however, resides a persistent responsibility, and it is this:

How else can I deploy these resources? Who else requires security and assistance? How best can I achieve what I was meant to achieve when it comes to helping others?

Politically, I call myself a compassionate and fiscally conservative Republican, who believes that the government should not come into the home. I try to conduct my philanthropic activities within that framework.

I learned this behavior from life and I learned it from my friends, Christian and Jewish. These friends were some of the other role models along the way who taught me the importance of leaving the world a better place than you found it.

Jewish people who found their way to the United States and succeeded here have a history of giving, and many Cubans who found their way to the United States have learned a lot from that.

Both of these groups not only are immigrants — we also are refugees, and sometimes that can be a difficult experience to overcome. Someone who is in a new land — well, when you arrive with nothing and then you get something, sometimes you don't want to let it go. Giving is really a learned experience. You need to learn how to give, because the natural instinct is to keep.

I have worked to learn how to give, and I think I'm getting pretty good at it. Over the years, I have made significant donations to children's hospitals and foundations, to The Early Childhood Initiative Foundation, and to other groups at home and abroad.

I am reluctant to name all the recipients. It smacks of puffery. That is not why I do these things. I don't want to dwell on this, but I'm also active on a more one-on-one basis.

It just became something that I enjoyed. I have a deep sense of gratitude for the blessings of this country, which has given us so many opportunities, and this is how I repay some of that debt I feel.

Sometimes, I help someone with whom I come into contact or someone I've heard about. For instance, I recently covered the tuition for a young man who goes to a private high school. I knew the boy, and he had written me an eloquent letter. His dad was out of a job; the school carried Salvador for as long as it could, but he had to leave, though he loved that school. I told the school, "Look. I'll pay his tuition going forward."

In this case, I did make a point and I'm still making it. I stay in touch with Salvador and I say, "Remember what was done for you. It will be your turn one day to do this for somebody else."

So, again, this is why I share these things. This is why I'm writing this book. I want and expect my children and their children to follow my lead in these matters, and I hope this book will instill these ideas in other people.

Maybe somebody I have yet to meet — or never will meet — will read this and pick up on what I'm saying and will decide to do something. In the popular phrase of the day: Carry it forward.

But please also understand this: It really makes me feel good to do these things. In some ways, these are selfish acts because of the profound satisfaction I derive from doing them.

OCTOBER 3

Santo Domingo

After several arduous days, I decided to treat myself at Parador de Santo Domingo de la Calzada, originally a 12th-century public hospital that often treated pilgrims who had become ill during their journeys. Today, it's one of the best resting places in this region. It is almost in the center of town, across from a beautiful cathedral and tower. After checking into a room, I rested in a hot bathtub until I fell sleep, right there. My feet, back and every bone in my body ached. Most importantly, the hotel provided laundry service, and I had everything in my bag washed and dried. I felt so clean!

Just a block from the hotel was a popular, pedestrian-friendly street, full of shops and tapas bars. It was here that I met my next trail companions, two nurses from Madrid and a writer from Scotland.

I was especially touched by Stephen, the writer from Scotland. He was going through a difficult period in life. Economically, he was starving and his clothing showed it, but spiritually, he was one of the richest people I have ever met. He spoke fluent Spanish with a Castilian accent. After all, he had studied in Madrid and had remained there after graduation to become a teacher.

This was a very special person. He knew more about this journey and the region than I did; he seemed to be a walking encyclopedia. During one of those special moments when the nurses — Nuria and Jema — and Stephen and I were within talking distance of each other, we had an amusing conversation.

At one point, the nurses looked at each other and said, "Should we ask him?" They laughed, and one of them said, "The first day we saw you, we said to each other, 'This guy is rich.' Are we right?"

I could not help but smile. I asked them what in the world made them think that? I had not told anyone along the way anything about what I did for a living or refer to my resources in any way.

They said that it was something about the way I conducted myself. "Rich people carry themselves differently," one of them said. "There are those who pretend to be rich, but one can tell they are imposters. The really rich ones are different."

I immediately flashed back to my days at Xavier High School and those trips to hear the Philharmonic. Maybe I was right after all. Maybe I did learn a lesson by studying the patrons at those Lincoln Center concerts.

Somewhere along the way, Stephen also offered a statement from the heart.

"People ask, *'Donde esta la España que amo?'* [where is the Spain that I love?], and I have found it. It is not in the large cities. It's in the country-side, where we are."

He mused about the generous and kind nature of the "simple people" we had encountered. As it often happens, when I left his side today, I did not think I would see Stephen again.

I was to be proven wrong.

OCTOBER 4
Villafranca Montes de Oca

Today, I temporarily left El Camino so I could engage in another type of journey, one that started decades earlier when I met Father Vincent Duminuco, my mentor from so many years ago at Xavier High School.

This side trip took me to the small town of Loyola, in the Basque country, for the next few days. In this small village lies a magnificent cathedral in honor of Saint Ignatius of Loyola, the founder of the Jesuit order. Surrounded by verdant mountains and under a flawlessly blue sky, I arrived at this place.

I had lost contact with Father Vincent from the time I left Xavier until one of my sons, Alex, graduated several years ago from another Jesuit institution, Belen Jesuit Preparatory School in Miami. Much to my surprise, the keynote speaker at the graduation was Father Vincent. He had come a long way since our days in New York.

As the ceremony ended and families began to depart, I made my way to the stage from where he had shared the same profound values he discussed with me almost 30 years earlier. As I made my way past the others on stage, I reached then-principal Father Marcelino Garcia, and I extended my hand to Father Vincent.

Father Marcelino began to introduce me as "Mike Fernandez," but Father Vincent reached for my hand and, much to my surprise, said, "Miguel Fernandez, I knew my thoughts about you would be validated, especially as I walked into the school's administration building and your name was above the main entrance." At this point, his handshake turned into a hug.

Now, so many years after our first encounters, he was not as tall as I

"The painted scallop shell represents the pilgrimage. All the lines on the shell (the trails) lead to one place. The staff is a reminder that we all need something to lean on."

had remembered. Since I had last seen him in 1972, Father Vincent had moved to higher positions within the Jesuit order. This time, I was determined not to lose touch again. So, during the next few years, we communicated via email.

Then, one day, I received an overnight package from him. It was a crucifix with a short note: "I am ill. I know I can trust you to take this back to my home in Loyola." He passed away in 2008.

Now, here in Loyola at last, I found myself outside this wonderful cathedral and looking for the priest in charge. I walked into the parish church and asked for the lead Jesuit, only to be told that he would return the next day and would conduct the last Mass of the day.

Discouraged and disappointed, I walked around the grounds and found a place to spend the night. The next day, as I waited until the last Mass was conducted, I had the opportunity to visit the home of Saint Ignatius, where he lived as a son of a prominent family and was trained to serve in the military. This also is where he recovered after being severely wounded by the French in the Battle of Pamplona in 1521.

At around 6 p.m., as I sat on a bench outside the rectory, I was approached by an elderly Jesuit. I told him that I had a mission to complete by placing in his hand a crucifix given to me by his fellow Jesuit, Father Vincent Duminuco.

Much to my surprise, he told me that he knew Father Vincent. He invited me to join him in a small chapel, where he, the other Jesuits and a visiting priest participated in Mass. This was the same room in which Saint Ignatius had prayed.

This was an emotional moment.

The main building at the Sanctuary of Loyola — "completing my mission that started in 1968 at Xavier High in New York City."

CHAPTER**SIX**

DOING GOOD BUSINESS, DOING GOOD WORK

"Every business deal has to be a win-win. Never squeeze the last penny out of it. Make sure the other guy is happy."

If you're reading this book, you may already know this. But, for the record:

I am chairman and CEO of an investment firm based in Coral Gables, Florida. I, along with partners Jorge Rico, Luis Gonzalez, Marcio Cabrera, our CFO Isabel Peña and, sometimes, Peter Jimenez, focus exclusively on the healthcare industry. As I write this, we own majority interests in various firms in the healthcare space. They encompass many areas, from insurance companies to the manufacturing of vitamins.

For the most part, we have built the business by buying medium-size, profitable companies with at least $5 million in annual earnings. By investing in profitable businesses, we greatly reduce our risk. Once we control the company, we strengthen the balance sheet, invest in operational improvements and sometimes make adjustments in management — all with a view toward making the firm the "best of breed."

After a few years, we generally sell the improved firm to a public company. (I never had much appetite to run a publicly traded company, but I have invested in many during my professional life.) When the transaction is complete, my team and I find other things to do, other segments of the healthcare business within which to invest, and we do it again. We have been blessed 95 percent of the time, but we have had a few losers — and I have made my share of mistakes.

In summary: We profit by finding the niches that the big companies don't see or find too cumbersome to develop. We identify the niche, build or fix the company, grow it and then sell it. But we also always make sure that the employees who helped us fix the company remain secure in their positions.

We have built or restructured 24 companies, operated and/or managed them, and sold 11 companies, with virtually all these transactions becoming profitable. Our team has developed a system that works, and I will share much of it with you here — because I am, after all, writing a book about lessons learned during this, my life.

For ease, I've summarized our system under what I call the SUPER formula:

The warmth of family and character: "Lobo and me in the office. My personality?
Relaxed on the outside; focused on the inside."

THE SUPER FORMULA

SACRIFICE — We've already discussed this one. Do not expect immediate gratification. Don't be afraid to fall and to fail. This is how you learn. I don't think any company we've bought has ever ended up being quite what we thought it would be. We always analyzed it, invested an adequate amount of capital in it, and trimmed it when necessary. Then, we focused on what was left and built it into a segment leader.

URGENCY – We also talked about this. Do what others do, but faster. Our teams work as hard as humanly possible to beat our competitors to the reward. You should, too. You have one life. Use it to the max. This life is not a dress rehearsal.

PASSION – You must have passion. You must love what you do. If you don't like what you're doing, move on. Find something that lights you up in the morning. As a businessman, let me tell you something: After nearly four decades in business, I still look forward to Monday. To me, Monday is the day I get to play.

EXECUTION – It's the little stuff that matters. In building and selling every company, we have had a great deal of fun, and we tried to make money for our team of investors and operators. This was important. We never had a "job." We always had a mission. We've always been majority shareholders. Today, we own a variety of companies with thousands of employees and total revenues in the billions.

From the beginning to this moment, it's always the details that matter.

Take one of our retail businesses — I don't go to management meetings there because, you know what, they just tell me what they think I want to hear. Instead, I check the store bathrooms. If they're dirty, the managers aren't doing their jobs. I spend 20 minutes a week listening to customers on the phone. Then I go to the company's executives and I say this is wrong and that is wrong. They can't deny it. I've seen it with my own eyes and heard it with my own ears. Management may not like that I don't follow the organizational chart or the chain of command, but I prefer to deal directly with the people who are "touching" the customer.

RESULTS — There's always a way to accelerate the growth. All these companies had a common denominator — we found a way to accelerate the growth. For a company we started in Tampa, I engaged the great actor James Earl Jones to serve as our spokesman. He has an impeccable reputation and a very recognized presence. He gave us credibility. The result? We went from breakeven to serious profitability in four months. Always look for a way to accelerate your growth. And remember, it isn't revenue that's important — it's earnings.

Making Every Deal a Win-Win

This also is important: Every business deal has to be a win-win. That is, it must be a win for each side, and sometimes that means more than two sides.

I'll give you an example. In 2002, we acquired a company that was insolvent. We paid $28 million. The company was losing $60 million a year. We had it at breakeven in a few months. How do you go from a $60 million loss to breakeven so quickly? Simple. You have to align incentives.

In this business, which we renamed, we had hundreds of doctors and we contracted with many hospitals and thousands of specialists.

Someone else may have looked at the company and seen a business in which the professionals worked for the owners. We had a different philosophy. Our view of the business was that we worked for the physicians, because they were the people who saw and touched patients. Every time a hospital admission was ordered or a prescription was written, these doctors were in control of our expenses. As a business, we received money from the customers, but it was the healthcare professionals who had control of our expenditures.

We needed them to understand how money was being spent and the consequences of those expenditures, not only for the business but also for them and for their patients. We could not, and we would not, tell them how to practice medicine, but we could provide information as to how their actions affected the outcome of their patients' health.

We called all of them into a meeting and we said, "Look, we just bought this company, and we want all of you to be part of it. So the good news is, I'm going to give you 20 percent of the company. But as partners, you have to understand how to spend the money."

Treats for a cow!

120

Accepting a challenge: "I made a bet that I could make a cow 'kiss' me. It took a few weeks at our home near Tallahassee. First I had to get the cow to trust me by giving her treats. Then I had to get close enough to have a cookie taken off my lips. I won the bet."

MY 20 TOP TIPS FOR SUCCEEDING IN BUSINESS

1. Recognize your customer. It's the best lesson I ever received.

2. Never forget that you never build anything by yourself. Share the credit; share the wealth. I have been very fair with the team that works with me. These managers tend to go with me from company to company. I trust them; they trust me.

3. Ask a question of someone before leaving work each day. Do you need anything? Can I do something for you?

4. Treat others at least as well — or even better than — you would expect them to treat you.

5. Be hard on the issues, but soft on the people.

6. Before you ask someone to do something, do it yourself if you can.

7. In the long run, the good guy always wins.

8. Don't try to invent. Instead, improve upon what already has been created.

9. Never sit at the head of the table. If you do, people will be intimidated and will tell you only what they think you want to hear.

10. When meeting with someone in your office, get up from behind the desk and sit next to him or her. Why? See No. 9.

11. Don't allow anyone to define you.

12. Set your goals at seemingly unreachable levels.

13. Identify mistakes quickly.

14. Embrace failure. This is how you learn.

15. Give of yourself.

16. Give back to the community and to the world in which you live.

17. Leave this world a better place than when you arrived.

18. Make sure to have a partner — a spouse or other special person who understands, appreciates and supports your goals.

19. If a job does not fulfill you, look for one that will.

20. Be grateful. Show it.

We didn't do anything — not one single thing — to inhibit good care for our patients, but we asked the doctors to at least consider the cost of tests, surgical suites in outpatient settings, the sort of things that wouldn't compromise care.

We also looked closely at the company, and we looked at the niches. It had 22,000 (older) Medicare patients and more than 100,000 (younger) commercial patients. We gave up the 100,000 commercial patients and referred them to other insurance companies that were better equipped to serve their needs. A few of our investors asked, "Are you kidding? We will lose over $200 million in revenue."

I said, "The earnings are irrelevant if the outcomes for the patients' health are not improved. This model, based on the specialists and the doctors who partner with us, should be focused on the expertise of the doctors. Most of these doctors are older and they are best suited to serving older patients, not young families. And, when the day comes that a buyer wants to acquire this company, the price will be based on earnings, not revenue."

"WE WERE FOCUSED AND WE HAD A MISSION — TO BE THE BEST HEALTH PLAN FOR OLDER CUSTOMERS."

So, we sacrificed more than $200 million in revenue, but we now were focused and we had a mission — to be the best health plan for older customers.

Basically, we knew how to focus on earnings, the doctors knew how to focus on care and patient outcomes. The key was to make those doctors our partners, and it wasn't all that complicated.

So, in 2005, we signed a deal to sell that company to a national insurance company for $485 million. Pretty nice return there — buy it for $28 million, improve patient care, don't be greedy, share the pie with key partners, and sell it 2½ years later.

It took three or four months for the deal to close, and during that time, our earnings rose from $60 million to $72 million. As a result, some of my partners thought we should renegotiate the deal with the buyer and raise the price.

I said, "No. We have a deal for $485 million. It's a good deal for them, and we don't

Crossing into Spain from France: "I still had 480 miles to go."

Never cross the "border" from good to bad business practices to pursue profits. Allow them to be informed by your humanity, faith in people and responsibility to help others.

want to sell them a company at its peak. We want to sell them a company that's growing, because, sooner or later, they will buy something from us again."

I've never done a deal thinking that it's my last deal. Never squeeze the last penny out of it. Make sure the other guy is happy. If he's happy, I'm happy.

When I got into business, my goal was to make $1,000 a year for every year I was old. So, at age 30, I would want make $30,000 a year; at age 40, I would want make $40,000, and so on. Well, it turned out to be a lot better than that.

Thirty-five years ago, my great friend Cesar Alvarez, now co-chairman of the 1,750-attorney Greenberg Traurig law firm, told me something that is very wise: Focus on the big numbers, not the little ones. So, if I invested $28 million and I'm selling it for $485 million, what's another $20 million for me? It doesn't change anything. Focus on the $485 million, and why take the chance of upsetting them?

And by the way, they did come back, and we have done other business with them during subsequent years.

Reputation Before Ruthlessness

Someone recently asked me if I'm ever ruthless in business. The answer is no. I don't believe in it. Reputation is 51 percent of doing a deal, and I nurture and safeguard my reputation before, during and after every transaction.

It was my reputation that helped me persuade James Earl Jones to work with us in 1994, and it was my reputation and friendship with Pat and Chris Riley that helped me forge an ongoing alliance with basketball great Earvin "Magic" Johnson, now a successful businessman and humanitarian.

We're working together now on a project that, through one of our companies, brings comprehensive medical care to HIV/AIDS patients. The focus from day one has been the same as the focus in all our other businesses — how can we develop a niche that is unrecognized by our competitors, while improving the care and quality of life for our patients, and generating a reasonable profit?

Earvin is larger than life, and I am not referring to his height. His signature smile, unique laughter and obvious sincerity about everything he touches make him — wait for it — lovable! My friend Earvin is a gift to mankind.

Why would Magic Johnson invest his greatest asset — his reputation, his "brand" — in an individual who has close to zero knowledge of sports, whom he had met just once and who happens to be in an industry often accused of employing questionable ethical

Earvin (Magic)
Johnson and my
son Cristofer at a
Miami Heat game.

127

practices? The short answer is: My lifetime of building goodwill, a good reputation, a perception of kindness and a proven track record (along with personal chemistry).

Still, none of this means that I do business with everyone I meet.

If I don't like somebody, I don't do business with him or her. The numbers are inconsequential. I don't care what they're willing to pay. If there's a gut feeling that's not good, it's not going to get good. Bad people ultimately will hurt you. This approach

Mike Fernandez is among the greatest men I've met. His belief in his fellow man, his commitment to his family, and his astute understanding of how to make a profit — all the while leaving people and communities better off — are rare and special traits.

Surely I am blessed that my good friend and former coach, Pat Riley, introduced me to him. Mike is honest, smart, caring and committed, and we both have built businesses on the principles of doing well and doing good. Since we joined forces, Mike has become a brother and mentor to me.

I played on the best basketball team ever assembled, the 1992 Olympic Dream Team. Know this: If I were asked to start a dream team of entrepreneurs, my first selection would be Mike Fernandez.

Earvin "Magic" Johnson
BUSINESS PARTNER AND NBA LEGEND

and this attitude were not developed after I had a few dollars safely tucked away. This was my practice even when I could not rub two pennies together.

I've walked away from more deals than you can imagine. There was an investor who wanted to acquire something we had, and we talked, and it finally came to the point where I said, "With all due respect, I just don't click with you, and I really don't want to go down this road because, even though this is our first meeting, the chemistry is not right. You're going to dislike me, and I'm going to be regretting it, so I'd rather not do this."

He was in shock. His ego was punctured. He was not used to being turned down on any deal, especially by a person half his age. He said, "Do you have any idea how much money you're turning your back on?"

I said, "It doesn't matter. I have a little bit of money, so I'm okay. I just don't want to go down the path you are suggesting."

But when it all works out, the human rewards are so wonderful. Here's an example of that: When we sell one of our companies, we — as the lead investor — distribute substantial sums not only to management but also to all deserving members of the enterprise. To date, the sum of these distributions exceeds $100 million. Some employees have received bonuses of as much as a year's pay, and a few received even more than that.

So, one day, I'm having coffee in a Cuban place in Miami and a lady comes up to me and says, "Excuse me, are you Mike Fernandez?" I said, "Yes." And she says, "Awwww." And she gives me a big hug, and I have no idea who she is. She says, "I came from Cuba in the 1960s and I've worked as a maid in a hotel in South Beach all of these years. Because of your generosity to my daughter who worked for you, I was able to stop working and stay home and take care of my grandchildren, so I want to thank you."

Those moments are so rewarding. Managing your business as if you are managing your reputation is good for business and it can lead to performing good deeds.

You want to talk about the bottom line? A real bottom line?

Here it is: It can be done.

Indeed, your business practices should be informed by your humanity, by your faith in the goodness of people, and by your responsibility to help others. Feeling good IS the bottom line!

OCTOBER 5

Burgos

For a change, the weather improved as I rejoined El Camino. By coincidence, it was a holiday weekend, the feast in honor of El Cid, a medieval nobleman and military leader who became famous for fighting the invading Moors. Spain's national hero, he was born in a small town near Burgos.

This was a special treat. Not only were people dressed as traditional town folk, but others were dressed as knights in armor and on horseback.

This also served as a surprising — and welcome — reunion with some people I had met on the trail. A doctor and his wife from California, Stephen (the writer from Scotland), Jema and Nuria (the nurses from Madrid), and others. Through a weird coincidence, of all of the places to eat in Burgos, we all ended up that evening at the same tapas bar.

My three Camino friends were staying in the "albergues" (inexpensive and often crowded hostels) and I felt guilty that I was spending the night at the best hotel in town, in need again of the laundry service.

We were a short walk from the hostel, just across a small bridge that leads you out of the historic section of Burgos. After a good meal, we were about to leave, for they needed to find their place for the night, when I asked them to walk with me to my hotel. Not one of them uttered even a word of complaint. Within a few minutes, we were there. We entered the lobby and, by the look in their eyes, I could tell that this type of accommodation was foreign to them.

I asked them to wait for a moment while I walked to the front desk. It was our lucky day; the place had only two available rooms. I asked the clerk to charge those rooms to my credit card. He handed me two keys, which

I carried as I walked 10 steps to where my friends sat. I handed them the keys.

At first, they did not understand. Then, they refused. But I employed my best white lie: "It's already paid for and if you don't use it, the hotel will have two empty rooms and you will not be on a soft bed, with fresh linens, a private bath, a tub and privacy." They hugged me and accepted.

It was a great evening, as we agreed to clean up, rest for a while and meet later and go out for a substantial dinner. Tonight, there were at least three happy pilgrims in town.

First view of Burgos, Spain. An ancient city and the home of El Cid, the Spanish knight who led the successful fight against the Moors. "Here I would enjoy the biggest steak I have ever consumed — all of it!"

OCTOBER 6

Castrojeriz

It was a long and silent walk from Burgos to this small town of Castro-jeriz. The town itself seems rather inconsequential, but what stood out was the empty shell of a Templar castle on the closest hill. With a commanding view of miles in every direction, it must have been magnificent in its days of glory.

The town can be seen from miles away as the meadows begin a gradual slope downward. A scarcity of trees (and shade) makes this section rather monotonous, but the body soon syncs with the brain, which for days has been in tune with each step and with the sound of my walking stick as it taps the ground.

My mind is blank. My conscience is clear. I am one with this journey.

I have become desensitized to the inconveniences of life as a pilgrim. Actually, although I am tired and uncomfortable, I have embraced the journey's tranquility, its simplicity. A transformation has occurred and I hope it lasts.

I don't quite understand it, but I am at peace and my heart feels like it's beating slower than it ever has beaten. My eyes are focused on the horizon, as the Templar castle that distinguishes this town enlarges with every step taken.

Is it possible that in the middle of nowhere between Burgos and Castro-jeriz I am actually noticing a change? Is this the miracle that a pilgrimage is said to bring to the pilgrim?

Church of Santa Maria del Manzano, Castrojeriz, Spain: *"I wasn't allowed to take any pictures inside, but they were willing to take a euro donation!"*

CHAPTER**SEVEN**

BOOTS ON THE GROUND — MY BUSINESS BOOTS

"You must know what the customer wants and expects."

One of the greatest business attributes with which I have been blessed is the ability to recognize, even leverage, my weaknesses. That, in turn, helped me develop a non-so-phisticated, common-sense approach to business.

I always thought that most people recognized their weak points and, to compensate for them, surrounded themselves with experts who could fill the gaps. Today, I am still surprised by how many leaders feel so threatened that they avoid hiring people who they think may be smarter than they are. In my case, I have so many weaknesses that I often admit publicly that I consider myself "the dumbest person in the room."

Over the years, I've repeatedly seen people who, even when they recognized their weaknesses and hired the right people to offset those weaknesses, still would not truly succeed. Hiring an expert means little if you don't get out of the way and let that person do his or her job. Sometimes, your ego can be a powerful enemy that works against your own success.

During my nearly four decades in business, I've seen smart people make the fatal mistake of micromanaging their subordinates rather than focusing on the big picture. This was especially true if the leader had succeeded in a prior venture. If not properly managed, the ego can override common sense.

Taking the High Road

Here's an example:

I knew a very successful physician who sold a terrific medical practice by the time he was in his mid-30s and decided to get into another business. He came to see me, hoping that I would invest in his new business. Excuse me for saying this, but I have found that, with just a few exceptions, physicians make poor business leaders. It could be their sense of self-assurance, an understandable professional hazard of being a person who makes life or death decisions every single day.

Anyway, I met with this physician years ago, and he seemed tense and combative after presenting a business idea that he thought was brilliant. I did not agree with him — not because it wasn't a good idea, but because the business model and service had very few barriers to entry. That is, anyone could duplicate it.

After an hour-long meeting, I politely turned him down. He was upset, as if I had attacked him. He told me that he had read about me and knew that I had never graduated from college. He, on the other hand, had graduated with honors and then spent additional years in medical school. He went on to tell me that the system had to be rigged to benefit those who cheated or engaged in illegal behavior. How else, he wondered, could someone (like me) who did not complete a formal education earn more than he did?

I took the high road, wishing him a good day and good luck.

He failed to understand that, though our investments are in the healthcare field, we succeed or fail based on a business model that can be replicated and grown. This magnitude of success can never be based on the talents (and limitations) of a single person. We historically have enjoyed a high level of financial reward due to scalability — providing services to the masses — and that, by the way, created jobs. As a practicing physician, he employed four or five people to support his operations; our companies employed hundreds or sometimes thousands of people.

I wish that he had been familiar with one of my favorite quotes, from Henry Ford: "Wealth, like happiness, is never attained when sought after directly. It comes as a byproduct of providing a useful service."

What the Dinosaurs Taught Me

Allow me to go back to where this section began.

We have hired many people, and the most important thing that has allowed us to grow and expand our reach is that we actually allow these professionals to employ their expertise. We expect that mistakes will be made, but that these executives have the intelligence and good street sense to correct those mistakes (and learn from them) or to ask for assistance.

I deeply appreciate and respect the expertise these senior managers employ to create value for our customers, our employees and our investors. But value also can be greatly expanded and reinforced through a "feet on the ground" approach.

"I HAVE FOUND A BETTER WAY — BY PLACING YOURSELF IN THE CUSTOMER'S SHOES."

The old adage about "managing by walking around" applies not only to strolling down the office corridors. I have found a better way — by placing yourself in the customer's shoes.

I learned the value of this practice long before I started building my own businesses. It started when I was in high school and working in that souvenir kiosk at the American Museum of Natural History in Manhattan. I had no obvious incentive to step out from behind the counter at which I sold the museum's trinkets, but I did have sufficient natural curiosity to know what the visitors to the century-old institution were doing while there.

We sold plastic dinosaurs, key chains, camera film, plastic bone–like parts of animals, postcards and other items. I found it surprising that, though we had plastic dinosaurs of nearly all types, we did not offer a plastic brontosaurus, which was the

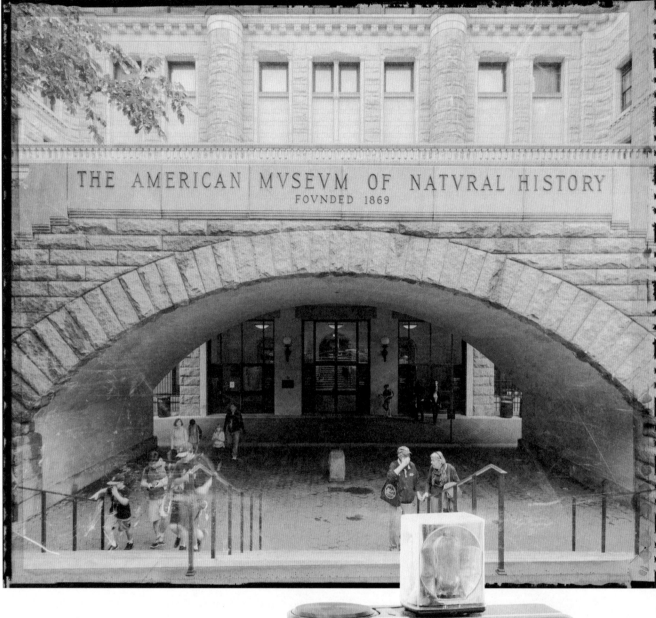

THE AMERICAN MVSEVM OF NATVRAL HISTORY
FOVNDED 1869

I kept all the profits from my 25 cubed flash-bulbs. I doubled my investment.

largest and most impressive exhibit in the whole place. In addition, though we sold film, we did not sell flashbulbs. At the time, most small cameras were produced by Kodak, and they generally had space for a small, four-sided flash cube that would revolve every time users snapped photos.

After a few weeks, I mentioned to my manager that this must be an oversight, as it did not make sense that we would sell film and not flashbulbs (after all, the pictures were taken indoors) and, moreover, that we did not sell a brontosaurus model. She stared at me with something approaching disbelief, apparently puzzled by my statement. After what seemed like an eternity, she said, "We know," and then turned away.

After a few more weekends . . . still no flashbulbs, still no brontosauruses. Wow. I realized that she simply had no incentive to be more productive. She collected her modest salary whether or not we sold flashbulbs or brontosauruses. It made no difference to her.

So, before long, I went into the storage room and found the name of the distributor of the plastic dinosaurs and the film. I wrote down the address and found the place in Brooklyn.

Using my own money from my salary, I purchased 100 plastic brontosauruses and 25 of those cubed flashes. I could barely contain myself. I could not wait to find out if my business instinct was right. It seemed like another eternity, but Saturday finally came. I entered the museum with my two boxes and laid out the products in the display. By Sunday, I was sold out, and no one in management noticed what I had done. I was barely 15 years old.

The following day, I took a different route home and passed by the museum. I wanted to tell the manager what I had done. I thought she would be as thrilled as I was. After all, this was newfound money for the institution. I made my way to the small office where she worked, only to learn that it was her day off.

So, instead, I proudly told her boss what I had done. Not only did he not appreciate it, but he reprimanded me for breaking the museum's rules.

I clearly was the only winner here. I had learned the importance of personally discovering and serving the customers' needs. I also learned that incentives need to be aligned in order for everyone to be pulling in the same direction. Lastly, I learned that it's not always bad to fail to follow the organizational chart or the chain of command. Breaking the rules is not always bad, and, in fact, it can be very good — so long as one is not also breaking the law.

MISTAKES QUITE OFTEN LEAD TO SUCCESS

"Failure doesn't mean you are a failure. It just means you haven't succeeded yet."
— **ROBERT H. SCHULLER**

That quote from Robert H. Schuller, a noted pastor, evangelist and motivational speaker, is one of my favorites, because it touches on a personality characteristic that is important to me — tenacity.

At a recent awards ceremony, I was introduced by the organization's leader, who mentioned my various business successes. Though appreciative of the praise, I considered this "uneven reporting." As I stepped on stage, I decided to address this lack of balance, because, after all, I knew that I made more than my share of mistakes along the way and they proved essential to my ultimate success.

Among those mistakes, failures and shortcomings:

- I was at best a C student in high school.

- I attended college for one semester before dropping out.

- While in the Army, I was promoted twice and demoted twice.

- I crashed my first car the same day I got it. Five years later, I also crashed my second car.

- I failed at my first marriage and at my second marriage.

- I ignored my health and ended up with two heart attacks, prostate cancer and other issues.

- I failed at my second business and had to move in with my parents for three years — along with my first wife and first two sons.

- We lost millions in a home-nursing business. We lost money in lots of businesses before we began to get it right.

- I was filled with self-doubt and often became depressed, sometimes for weeks, before I would push myself to snap out of it.

Well, you get the point. Tenacity. I just never gave up. Never. Never.

All these mistakes led to successes beyond my wildest expectations.

I have been happily married for 15 years. I have five wonderful children for whom I would do anything, including saying no when necessary. We succeeded in multiple business ventures. I have some genuine friends — people on whom I can count. I've been able to help hundreds of people, sometimes strangers, simply because I was in the right place at the right time.

So . . . on we go!!!!

Up, up and away ...
Michelle and me in
the Starship. Our
first twin-engine
plane.

Chapter 7

One of the greatest business attributes with which I have been blessed is the ability to recognize, even leverage, my weaknesses.

"*I was in this village during siesta time. I slept a little here, but siestas are not really my style.*"

The bottom line: I kept all the profits from my 100 brontosauruses and 25 cubed flashbulbs. I doubled my investment, just as my father had with that first batch of leather coats.

Three Business Principles Above All Others

As an adult, I have benefited in business from what I learned from my father and from my actions at the museum. I also realized that these lessons were, in fact, eternal. So long as the customer is receiving perceived value in a convenient form, the customer is satisfied. But you must know what the customer wants and expects.

As we grew our companies over the years, I would apply these three principles above most others:

- If you want to know what the customer needs and wants, get out of the office.
- To execute your goal, pay close attention to the basics.
- Don't get trapped within the organizational chart.

In 2011, we acquired an insolvent insurance company that was brought to my attention by state regulators. They were concerned, if not already convinced, that the company was about to fail. We swiftly had to capitalize the company to industry standards, replace its management and invest in technology. We did all this.

Soon, one of my partners, Peter, had an idea: We should consider serving a specific group of patients — those who suffered from HIV/AIDS. By 2011, having this dreadful disease no longer meant that the patient was living under a death sentence. Medication for HIV/AIDS and the standard of care for these patients had greatly advanced.

We crafted a business model, and we created an insurance product. For the next seven months, our team developed relationships with doctors and hospitals that specialized in treating infectious diseases, and lined up all manner of services needed to serve our HIV/AIDS patients. This was a deviation from our past experiences, in which we dealt almost exclusively with older patients.

A large number of these new patients were on the state's healthcare program. Many of them were economically challenged. In addition, there was a high incidence of drug use and mental illness, as well as homelessness. All of this was new to us.

It was time to get my boots back on the ground. Summer arrived, and with it our usual two-month stay in the Bahamas. Phase One of my plan: I did not shave during those two months.

Upon my return in August, I put on my oldest pair of pants, a shirt that was way too large, and flip-flops. That was Phase Two.

Marcio Cabrera, my partner of more than 20 years, was responsible for the operations of the company that would own and manage this HIV/AIDS plant. As a "recovering accountant," he is as good as it gets. Like the rest of us in the partnership, he was a former operator and knew the insurance business inside out.

I called Marcio and asked him for the names of the top three medical clinics with which we would be working. These offices would provide medical care to our HIV/AIDS patients, while Marcio's operation would handle all administrative, audit, claims and marketing duties.

I drove to the first one — the Ultimate Phase of my plan: Today, I was going to be a patient. I would experience our soon-to-be-realized business model from the customer's perspective.

This particular clinic was in Miami Beach. I parked a few blocks away from the clinic and headed one block east to Ocean Drive, walking in my flip-flops in the dry sand. I also stretched out in the warm sand to make sure a few grains were in my hair.

Entering the clinic, I passed a set of double doors — of which only one would open. Inexpensive plastic chairs sat in the waiting room. The walls were covered with old, tattered posters warning of the dangers of spreading the disease through unprotected sex and shared hypodermic needles. The air conditioner was loud and pushed out semi-cold, semi-humid air.

To the left of the entrance, I saw a check-in desk behind a glass barrier (probably intended to prevent bodily fluids from reaching the front-desk clerk). Two other people sat in the room, presumably waiting to see a doctor or receive lab results.

As I checked in, I made it a point not to smile and to seem unfriendly, though not disrespectful. The clerk barely looked up when she acknowledged me. I said: "I want to be tested for HIV. Can you do that?" She replied: "Do you have insurance?" I told her that I did not, and I would be paying myself.

My learning curve began immediately,

Three weeks without shaving, weighing less — and still smiling.

145

and it sharpened quickly.

For instance, to attract patients to our health plan, our experts and our managers had developed benefits better than those offered by the state. But, while I was sitting outside the nurse's office, I overheard two staffers saying that, though it was the beginning of the month, they already had distributed all the free bus passes.

At first, I thought this was good news for us. One of our proposed new benefits was free taxi service to make sure that patients did not miss any doctor appointments. This seemed like a great idea — until I spoke to one of the nurses.

"Did you hear about a new health plan that is coming out that will offer free taxis for transportation?" I asked. She responded: "I did, and we are contracted with them, but it's a benefit few will use. They do have other good points on the plan, though."

I was stunned. What did she mean, it's a benefit that few would use? After further conversation with her, in a very indirect way, I realized how correct she was.

"THESE PATIENTS NEEDED MORE TENDER LOVING CARE AND ATTENTION THAN TYPICAL PATIENTS."

They would in fact not be using what we perceived as a great benefit, but you had to be a patient to understand why. Some HIV/AIDS patients believe they are stigmatized by the disease, and sometimes those with whom they live do not know they have it.

What would your partner, parent or neighbor think if you began to get free taxi rides two or three times a month? This could raise questions. In fact, they preferred to take the bus and just blend in without attracting unwanted attention.

Our experts and managers had never thought of this, because they reached all their conclusions from within the sterile corporate offices in which they worked. By stepping out and seeing actual conditions on the ground, in just one day I learned more than my colleagues knew about the services patients actually needed and wanted.

After visiting three locations, I knew enough to confront my team and make suggestions that would have enormous impact:

- Offer bus passes, not taxi services.

- Provide umbrellas because many patients stand in the Florida sun for long periods of time.
- Provide patients with home-cleaning services.
- Provide patients with food-delivery services.
- Coordinate psychiatric care.
- Assemble a group of people who look under bridges and in old buildings for patients we otherwise would not find. (Some of those we hired for this were HIV/AIDS patients and knew the ropes.)

These patients needed more tender loving care and attention than typical patients. Among other things, this meant that we had to staff our customer-service operations more deeply than usual, as these patients required much longer interactions because of their complications.

Let me clarify — many HIV/AIDS patients do not live in poverty. Some are lawyers, teachers, bus drivers, even celebrities. They are just like you and me. They want to be respected and treated just as I would want to be treated. Our health plan targeting this disease has now been shown to improve healthcare outcomes by providing preventive care and, through aggressive care management, we are reducing hospitalizations and managing comorbidities.

One of our companies had once again proven that we can do well while doing good for the communities we serve.

OCTOBER 7

Near Frómista

I am happy to share with you that I have completed a significant portion of my journey! Like the James Taylor song says, "I've seen fire and I've seen rain. I've seen lonely days that I thought would never end. . . ."

During the last two weeks, I have climbed mountains, walked for hours in rain and for what seems like an eternity in sun so hot that I searched for streams and fountains where I could dunk my head to cool off.

The funny thing is that I would not change one second of it. I have met interesting people from all over the world, including the writer from Scotland, the nurses from Madrid, a monk from Korea, and a doctor and his wife from California. This is among the best reasons to hike from one country to the next.

OCTOBER 8

Santa Maria church (1124 A.D.) in Villalcázar de Sirga

Look up and around this church. You have angels everywhere. See the angels?

Santa Maria: Carved in stone — ground to ceiling of the vaulted entry — hundreds of angels looked at each visitor.

CHAPTER **EIGHT**

REDUCE RISK: DON'T INVENT BUT REINVENT

"My big competitor had given me an insider's view of his operation and the market."

God knows that, in spite of my limitations, I have been repeatedly blessed. I'm sure that most readers would not want their children to lack, as I do, a formal college education. But I was able to offset that liability through the blessing of common sense. The following story illustrates this point.

One day, I asked Robert, a longtime friend and an extremely bright graduate of Harvard, why he had not started a business of his own. After all, he had an appealing personality, God-given abilities and plenty of common sense — attributes that he could apply outside of a large, cumbersome corporate culture.

His response surprised me. He danced around the answer for a few moments and then finally said: "As a lawyer, I usually look around and see mostly the downside risk. On the other hand, you, Mike, focus on the upside and rely on professionals like me to manage the risk. I worry too much."

He was partially correct. Because of my nature, I always tend to have a perspective that the glass is half full rather than half empty. Yet, I also am somewhat risk-averse, and I do search for the downside in any deal, and then thoroughly analyze it. The key is figuring out how to manage and limit the downside to make it part of the entire package and give it proper value in a business model.

Management of risk is very important to me and to any other businessperson, but this is not limited solely to matters of business. Risk management is applicable to every sector of life. Before you get married, maybe you should have a prenuptial agreement in place. If you have a boat, you need bilge pumps and other equipment to remove water if the hull's integrity is compromised — and life rafts if it turns out those bilge pumps are insufficient. Risk management is necessary in everything we do. If the risk is too high, don't get married, don't get in the boat.

Facing the Competition

So, now, with that understood, here is a story involving a very profitable — though risky — venture I entered into during the mid-1990s. I was in my 40s and already had enjoyed financial success to the point that I could slow down. Having sold previous companies to large national players, I had signed a non-compete agreement for three years in the South Florida market.

As had happened before, I contemplated retiring and enjoying life by spending more time with my family. I wanted to take a year off from work. Well, that's what I thought, but it did not work out. After just three weeks I felt like a caged animal. I simply am not wired to remain idle. At that point in my life, I couldn't even slow down.

At that point, I rented a small office, hired an assistant and began laying out the next business. It would be headquartered in Tampa, outside the area covered by the non-compete agreement.

The business blossomed, the years flew by, and then it was time to expand into the South Florida market, which represents more than 30 percent of Florida's population. Our major focus would be providing services to senior citizens.

But we faced a gargantuan competitor that would not easily allow us to enter this

Bridges in life: This one is along El Camino. "All of us need bridges to build better pathways for the challenges faced in both families and business."

market. The competitor was an international insurance company, and it controlled the majority of the market and clients that I was targeting.

Our team began preparing our entry into the Miami, Fort Lauderdale and West Palm Beach areas by expanding our network of physicians, hospitals and outpatient facilities. Six months later, we were ready to start hiring the last component that we needed before becoming operational and without which most businesses can't survive — the marketing and sales team.

It was at this moment that I received an unexpected telephone call from a well-respected lobbyist in the state capital who represented the biggest competitor. He asked me if I would meet with the chief executive officer of that company's southeastern region, which included Florida.

He had scotch and I drank water.

Always welcoming the opportunity to meet new people, I agreed. A few weeks later, I finally met that CEO for dinner at Caffe Abbracci, a fantastic restaurant in Coral Gables. I didn't know what to expect, but I was flattered that the "big shot" knew of me. As the conversation progressed, I was more flattered that he would even consider us, our little company, as a potential competitor.

After a social drink (he drank scotch and I drank water), we ordered dinner. Soon, he got down to business, though in a most cordial way. He was never antagonistic. He told me that the South Florida region was the most important market for his company, as the result of its large concentration of senior citizens. He told me that his firm had an aggressive sales organization that had proven itself by controlling the market for over a decade.

I even heard him say that the company spent more than $36 million a year in promotion and advertising, suggesting that a little company like ours might not

"I HAVE ALWAYS CONSIDERED MYSELF A GOOD (IF OFTEN LUCKY) SALESMAN."

be able to compete. He offered his advice, making certain to compliment us by mentioning that we had developed a good reputation in Central Florida in a short time. Bottom line, he offered the thought that I would be best served by focusing on growing our market share there — in Tampa and the rest of Central Florida, away from his market in South Florida.

I was flattered and challenged. But here's the thing: My big competitor had given me an insider's view of his operation and the market.

By taking the time to have dinner with me and by sharing his "wisdom" with me, this very nice big shot had validated our reasons to expand into South Florida. He also indirectly pointed to the fact that this was a "must-have" market for him. My conclusion: If we succeeded, this guy's company could be interested in buying us when we decided to sell and move on. But, most importantly, he told me about the effectiveness of his sales force. I have always considered myself a good (if often lucky) salesman,

Chapter 8

Built in Franco's time, this irrigation ditch furnishes life-giving water for many miles — and thousands of pilgrims — in an arid region of Spain.

At first, my body wanted to quit after six or seven hours, and I would cover no more than 10 miles. Now, after three weeks, I can cover 20 miles a day.

and that is a group of people with whom I can particularly connect.

Involuntarily, and in many ways, he shared information that was highly valuable to me.

After he finished his cordial and friendly scare tactic, I shared my view of the market. Though not as sophisticated as his operation and certainly much smaller, we had one advantage — a profound commitment to excellent customer service.

I pulled out my cellphone and asked him for the telephone number of his national customer-service department. I'm sure he must have thought it was a most unusual request — I could tell by the look on his face.

I called the number and placed my phone on speaker mode. Within a few rings, the call was answered by an automated voice: "Thank you for calling X. Your call is very important to us. Please stay on and someone will be with you." This message was repeated every 30 seconds or so. Our salad was served, we ate it, and they took away the plates before a person answered my call.

Then, I asked him to call our little company's customer-service department. He pulled out his phone and, before I gave him our number, I told him that if a live person did not answer his call within five rings, I would pay for the meal. He humored me by dialing the number. The call was answered within the first three rings.

This is what I told him — something that I believed with all my heart:

"In my prior businesses, we always have created value and a good costumer experience by first and foremost identifying and servicing our customers' needs.

"The person who calls us does not do so to congratulate us. People call us because they are not feeling well, or are worried about something, or possibly because they believe we have done something wrong. At our little company, the one area that we overstaff is the customer-service department, and it's open 24 hours a day.

"In addition, we align the incentives for the customer-service representative with the company's goals, by offering a weekly bonus that is earned if 98 percent or more of the calls are answered within the first three rings."

Then I got a little bolder, but with a smile. I added that it was our company's policy and my belief that we could take market share more by providing better service than by spending huge sums on advertising.

And so it went. During the next few years, we proceeded to take market share from all of our competitors — and we spent 90 percent less than they spent, all because of superior service.

But it's not only about service. Knowing that we could relate to salespeople and

It's been 35 years since I first met a young man named Mike Fernandez. Over the years, we've played many roles in each other's lives — lawyer, advisor, board member, friend, companion, brother. I've learned so much from him.

He's the very best example I've ever known of the self-educated man. He's deeply curious about so much, blended with an extraordinary capacity to focus attention and energies on literally anything that interests him — a new business, a relationship, philanthropy, boating, friends.

Is there a better listener? I haven't yet met that person. This great salesman understands how much you can learn by listening. He seeks out those who know a lot about any given subject, and listens intensely, absorbing all. This "human sponge" becomes truly expert. One good example: In the medical field, his success is legendary, and deservedly so. Not that very many years ago, he didn't even know what an HMO (health maintenance organization) was or how it worked. Today, he understands the subject better than anyone.

Most of all, he's my brother — albeit from another family — and my loyal and great friend for life. I am blessed to know him and to have him and his family in my life.

Cesar Alvarez
CO-CHAIR OF GREENBERG TRAURIG

their needs better than that CEO could, possibly somewhat isolated in his ivory tower, we targeted his sales team for hire. After all, the CEO told me that his firm had the best and most effective team in that market, and its large share of the market proved it.

That's all we needed to know. During the next 30 days, we hired the sales manager from my new friend's company and more than three-quarters of the sales team.

This is how we mitigated risk when facing competition from a formidable adversary. We also did not have to reinvent or start from scratch. We copied and slightly improved the benefits offered by our competitors, improved on the service they were providing to customers, and hired most of their sales team. As I've said: Don't invent, but reinvent by improving.

Postscript: A few years later, that regional executive of our largest competitor was promoted to CEO of the entire company. He now was responsible for all U.S. and international operations.

"WE SOLD OUR COMPANY — A $28 MILLION INVESTMENT THAT YIELDED $485 MILLION IN LESS THAN FIVE YEARS."

It was to him that we sold our company — a $28 million investment that yielded $485 million in less than five years.

When I met him again as we closed the deal, he said, with a smile: "Say all you want, but don't remind me about our dinner."

I never did.

Yes, 'I Am a Salesman'

At the most fundamental business level, I am a salesman, and I am immensely proud of that.

Regardless of whether you are presenting a new idea or concept, or making an argument in court, or offering your services as a surgeon, or addressing a crowd at a political rally, or possibly even selecting the next pope at the Vatican, a tremendous amount of selling is required and is taking place.

Think about it. Before a job is created for accountants or for customer-service people or pretty much anyone else, a salesperson did his or her job and a project proposed by that person got underway.

Without a politician selling an idea or a vision, no votes would be counted. Without a leader proposing and selling an initiative, no nation would take on the challenge. Without a coach's strategic plan and motivational selling of that plan, no team would win.

I remember having an opportunity to explain this view — to sell it — after a full day in Israel with Constance, George and Alex. We had been received as VIPs, including a private meeting with President Shimon Peres and shuttle rides between Tel Aviv and Jerusalem aboard military helicopters.

Finally, we were exhausted, and we retired to the Tel Aviv Hilton. Constance and I were getting ready for sleep when we heard a knock on the door. It was from George and Alex, my two oldest sons, and they had a serious look on their faces. One of them asked, "What the heck do you do?"

A good day at the office.

"Among our most memorable family trips — one where we learned so much was to Israel. President Shimon Peres and others welcomed Constance and me and our sons Alex and George. And we saw him in Miami, too."

At first, neither Constance nor I understood the question or its origin. Obviously, though, they were wondering why we were receiving these honors from the Israelis.

After a few seconds, I got it and, with a smile, I answered, as I have said all my life: "I am a salesman."

"You must do something else," one of the boys said. "You can't be just a salesman."

"Yes," I said, "that is all I am. All the blessings we have enjoyed, like the ones you have seen today, have been the product of not only what I have sold but also all of whom I have helped."

In order to advance, to get to the vision you have for a business or in personal life, you need to sell ideas. You need to persuade. You need to tell a story. I received a gift by understanding this at a very early age. You need to make an emotional connection, to build a bridge between you and the other side.

If you can make the emotional connection, that's when the sale occurs. In all fields of endeavor, if you can connect, you will accomplish your objectives and your dreams.

I consider it a gift to be able to connect emotionally with others — and the result of relevant connections is what I call a "sale." The initial contact will lead to a conversation, which leads to relevant and deeper understanding. The rest happens naturally.

We are the product and our words are the connector. I am a salesman who always has recognized that if you bring a solution, the rest is easy.

No more and no less.

OCTOBER 10

Calzadilla de la Cueza

It's incredible how the body will adjust, the body of a young man, an old man or an ill child. This journey has expanded my hope for children everywhere, especially those enduring a health-related crisis.

Just three months ago, I was training for this journey in Utah and I could barely make it through the day. A month later, I could do five or six hours in the mountains.

A new experience began when I took my first steps on the first day on El Camino. In the beginning days, my body wanted to quit after six or seven hours, and I would cover no more than 10 miles in tough terrain. Now, after three weeks, I can cover 20 miles a day, rest for the night and be ready for the next day with a smile.

Training and therapy are key for those in need! To the nurses and therapists who do this work, I commend you. I have found a new level of respect for the importance of the work you do.

Santa María Church in Carrión de los Condes, Spain: "As had happened before, a young priest asked for the pilgrims to stay after Mass. He asked each of us where we were from, and most said where they had stayed the evening before. But I said, 'Cuba,' and he then asked: 'Did you walk?' In humor I responded: 'If I did, it would be over water, and I would own this church!' He laughed; no one else did."

Orange 8:24 AM 81%

Carrion De Los Condes 43°
hourly

Wednesday		66°	43°
Thursday		66°	46°
Friday		61°	39°
Saturday		64°	39°
Sunday		63°	43°
Monday		63°	43°

Updated 10/9/13 8:24 AM

C H A P T E R **N I N E**

MY FAMILY, MY ASSOCIATES, MY SALVATION

"I am utterly blessed."

I believe we can be measured by the people who are closest to us, and in this I am utterly blessed.

I've already shared with you my parents' story. Here are sketches of some of the other people closest to me and most important to me: my wife, my children, my sister, my partners and my irreplaceable assistant.

Constance Margaret Tolevich, who would become Constance M. Fernandez, is my salvation, my rock and the single largest force for change in my life. When we began dating, neither of us wanted to get married, a fact that removed much of the pressure and expectation that accompany many other developing relationships. So, our relationship developed naturally and organically, without an artificial agenda. When we met during a business meeting, it was impossible to ignore Constance's physical beauty, as she was the most attractive woman I ever had met. What I could not anticipate at that moment was the magnitude of the beauty within her heart and mind — a beauty that enveloped even her everyday presence.

By 35 years of age, Constance did not have a child, and there was a reason for this. Born outside of Detroit in the town of Sterling Heights to a father who was a union worker at Ford and a mother who was a nurse, Constance endured a challenging childhood. Her parents divorced early and her mother was . . . difficult.

At early ages, Constance and her sister, Kim, found themselves caring for their two younger brothers, Alex and Michael. In essence, Constance and Kim were the parents in the household. They made breakfast, prepared paper-bag lunches for the boys, walked them to school and cared for them after school. The sisters rode bicycles to school every day and then pedaled back to care for their younger siblings.

After a few years of this, Kim was afflicted with leukemia. After a long struggle, she passed way. That left Constance as the sole parent figure in that household. These early experiences colored her attitude toward becoming a parent and, later, being a parent.

"CONSTANCE IS THE PARTNER THAT THE GOOD LORD WAS SAVING FOR ME, AND SHE CAME AS AN UNEXPECTED GIFT."

More happily, Constance's father, Alex, and his wife, Jean, are very close to Constance and Cristofer and to their other children and grandchildren. I am glad to say that Alex and Jean are loving retirement, are avid golfers, and enjoy tennis and walking.

I also brought some "baggage" into our relationship — two teenagers (George and Alex) and two younger children: Michelle, who was 7, and Michael, then 3. I did not make it any easier when, as the relationship progressed, I told Constance that — no matter what — those children always came first. I expected a backlash, but I received nothing but understanding and respect for my position. From day one, Constance bestowed protection, love and caring on each of the four — and on our family and household.

Here's an example: During one of our earliest dates, I asked her to join me at my South Florida home, where I was hosting a fundraiser for the Catholic Archdiocese of Miami. Constance had never been to my house, so I asked her to arrive 30 minutes

Constance: "The love
of my life today and
on our wedding day."

Grandpa T and Cristofer
relaxing at our Harbour
Island home.

169

My husband didn't ask me to do this, but I do acknowledge my "bias," admitting that I am not only the CEO of his fan club, but also his greatest cheerleader.

On meeting Mike, I was captured by his natural charm, innate intelligence, understated elegance and genuine humility. This man, who spent long days at the office in his suit, tie and cufflinks, had a personal life that needed mending. So I set out to repair this family and make a "house" a "home" for Mike and his children. That meant Wednesday family dinners, family vacations, gifts and birthday cakes. Slowly, we constructed — and united — a family. Then, Mike presented me the lifetime gift of Cristofer, child No. 5, to synergize the Fernandez clan.

I always tell Mike that he has "big shoulders," which is physically true, but also true is that he is a "grand caretaker" for so many. He is exceedingly generous, a man who comforts and indulges his loved ones to no end.

I love his accent, his tan skin, his dark hair and those big brown eyes. My love, sincere and loyal, is blended with respect and, yes, a measure of adoration.

Partly because I hold a business degree, his business prowess fascinates me, too. Many times, he will share a business experience with me, leading me to ask, "How did you know that?" His reply, in these words or similar: "Because that's the way it works!" He's a unique maverick, passionately driven to succeed every way he can.

Our very serendipitous union was destined to be. We complement and support each other in every way. Our best accomplishment? We agree — and celebrate — that we are more in love now than even on our wedding day 15 years ago.

Constance Fernandez

early. Naturally, she was right on time.

As I showed her around, I told her that, although I had more than 150 people coming for dinner, I would need to step out for about an hour to take Michelle to a recital at school. As a result, Constance would need to take charge of the dinner as hostess. Any other person would have walked out on me right there and then, but not Constance. The night went off without a hitch. When I returned an hour and a half later, she had made everyone feel right at home — in a house in which she did not even know where the bathrooms were!

Constance is the partner that the good Lord was saving for me, and she came to me as an unexpected gift. She is a fantastic stepmother, mother, daughter, sister, sister-in-law and more. I have told close friends that, based on her childhood, she could have turned out to be a total wreck or a complete angel.

Well, she is our angel. Only with her at my side have I found peace and happiness.

"My smiling brood: from left, Michael, Michelle, Cristofer, George and Alex."

"Our family two decades ago: Alex, Michelle and George — and me. In the middle is a proud father on the day when George (left) and Alex received their MBAs from the University of Miami."

George Michael and his family George is my oldest son. I am proud of his sense of giving and the manner in which he has embraced fatherhood. He is a better dad than I ever could have been. His wife, Lily, is a gift from God to my eldest, as she is sweet, caring, family-oriented and a terrific mother. Their daughters, Stella and Daniella, are blessed to have them. I have always referred to George as so generous that he "will give you his last shirt off his back." George graduated from the University of Miami and earned an MBA.

I am very proud of how George has grown from an introvert into a person who, as they say, is comfortable in his own skin. One of my proudest moments came during Alex's wedding as George spoke about his relationship with and love for Alex. When both were children, some of my fondest and happiest times came when I would pack a lunch and my father would drop me, George and Alex at a spot where Krome Avenue runs along the western edge of Miami. We would walk like vagabonds along the railroad tracks for three or four hours until we passed Tamiami Airport. When our walk was finished, I would call my father, who would pick us up. I don't think they remember much about our time walking and the stories I would tell them, but I do — and these memories are precious to me.

Alexander Michael and his family Alex is the second oldest, though he has traits similar to those found in a first-born child. He and George have been great, with only the minor challenges that come with all children. (I should know, as my mother reminds me that I was a challenge.) Alex's wife, Melanie, is an attorney who practices in Miami. Upon graduation, Alex chose to strike out on his own by getting a position with the largest healthcare and financial services turnaround firm in the nation. After three years there, he joined a technology startup. Friends tell me that Alex is very much like me and maneuvers well in any environment.

He always has been the most independent of the kids. I always could count on him for an engaging debate on any issue. (This kid really should have been a litigating attorney.) I welcomed those times, but not always, as some of these issues could be

Daniella and Stella: "Loving and, thank God, healthy."

stressful for both of us.

Like me, Alex appears to have some difficulty focusing too long on a single subject. I have learned to turn that into an asset, and I am sure he will, too. He also performs well under pressure.

One time, Alex, George and I were fishing on a boat about 20 miles south of Bimini when my back gave out. (As a result of my jumping out of planes in the Army, I have multiple herniated disks.) I could not move. I could not even sit up straight. While lying down in the cabin, I yelled instructions in the smallest detail regarding raising and securing the anchor, starting the engines, driving the boat, avoiding the shoals.

Alex and George got the boat safely back to Bimini. They performed perfectly and admirably under that pressure.

Michelle Esther Also referred to as "Mimi" by my family, Michelle receives all of the attention that the sole girl in a family of boys would be expected to receive. She physically resembles her mother, a woman to whom I was married for nine years. I never have met a girl as sweet as Mimi. We also have a special relationship, in that she is the only child who has taken a vacation with me but without the rest of the family. I have wonderful memories of her joining me on my first El Camino walk. She has never worked as hard in her life as she has worked while studying at Saint Thomas University School of Law. I have seen Michelle grow from a shy, timid and always smiling little girl into a secure, intelligent — and yes, still smiling — young woman.

For me, Mimi is a fountain of sweet memories: Long ago, as I drove her each day to Saint Thomas the Apostle Catholic School, she would slide down from her seat and hide under the car's dashboard as Mrs. Jennings would open the door at the curb. Mimi would look up, smile and extend her arm to allow her pre-kindergarten teacher to take her hand and guide her to class. Later, she flourished at Carrollton School of the Sacred Heart, where she was molded into the secure and outspoken young woman she is today. Then her studies took her to Holy Cross College and to the University of Miami, from which she graduated. Today, as I mentioned, she is busy in law school.

Mimi enjoys photography and, like my sister, loves animals. I have enjoyed our travels to Europe, Africa and, especially, our father-daughter trip to Paris. Still, our most memorable adventure was the 62-mile hike in Spain from Sarria to Santiago de Compostela.

At a time when few others occupied the trails, we bonded as she inquired about

"Michelle on a trip we took together to Paris. Above is Michelle and me fishing on the dock at Harbour Island in the Bahamas."

my childhood, and no topics were off limits. We crossed streams, hiked hills and walked red-clay, single-file trails defined on both sides by giant trees as a cold wind whirled about us. We talked when we wanted to talk, we walked in silence when we had nothing to say. I learned that, even with her ever-present smile, Mimi was strong physically and mentally. She could out walk me and outsmart me.

I am proud of her. I know that, just like me, she will make mistakes. But I also know that she has the backbone to spring back to her feet. Never underestimate my daughter's drive and determination.

Michael Brandon We joke that Mike somehow acquired all the athletic genes that might have been reserved for 10 generations of the Fernandez family. Humble with a sense of sacrifice and a passion for hard work, Mike naturally inspires people to respect him. He is as smart as he is fit. Just like George, Mike is a gentle soul, and he looks out for all in need. I remember how aware he was at an early age. While in the eighth grade he would ask me, "What car are you going to be driving when you pick

"SOMETIMES, WHEN I'M LYING DOWN, HE'LL THROW HIS 190-POUND MASS OF MUSCLE ON ME AND JUST HOLD TIGHT."

me up at school?" Then, he would ask me to drive up in the oldest car we had. I learned that he was aware that other kids had less than he did — and he did not want to hurt their feelings.

Here is a true story that further illustrates the point: At 81, my mom recently was hospitalized overnight with severe chest pains. Of course, she was visited by the grandchildren. But as the 4-foot-8, 102-pound matriarch awoke in the morning, she saw a bundle of blankets on a chair. Under it was Michael. After visiting her the night before, he went home and came back with a blanket and pillows. He was her guardian angel.

Michael is a hugger. Sometimes, when I'm lying down, he'll throw his 190-pound mass of muscle on top of me and just hold tight. Some of my favorite times were

My Father

My dad has to be the coolest guy I know. He does everything for me, even when he doesn't want to. My dad works really hard and is really good at what he does. My dad has this one facial expression that always gets me, my siblings and I call it "the looks". He always uses "the look" when we do something wrong, and he makes sure we don't do anything bad for a while. But he does it because he loves us. Also my dad and I spend a lot of time together, we go to the gym together and he walks while I play basketball, he also plays with me sometimes. We go on trips together all over the place, my favorite place is Tallahassee. My dad taught me how to shoot my first gun. This one time we went hunting and there were two hogs in front of us, he aimed, he pulled the trigger, and missed, them both! It was a funny moment. There are many more things I can write about my dad, but it would take up twenty pages to write. All I write to sum it all up is that, "he's the best".

Son Michael — then in the sixth grade — wrote this essay about his father. Here's Michael several years later, about to graduate from Belen Jesuit.

177

"Having a great time with Cristofer near our home in Park City, Utah."

walking with him on the beach in Harbour Island, the Bahamas, looking for driftwood and bringing it home. Or deer hunting at our Little River Plantation, where he managed to harvest two beautiful 10-pointers at almost sunset with two perfectly placed shots, just seconds apart. I know that Michael will continue channeling his focused energy and discipline toward a rewarding life.

Cristofer Miguel "C," as his mom calls him, is my only child with Constance. He is her treasure, and she dotes over him. We are told that he looks a great deal like his brother Alex, with his blondish/light brown hair and light eyes. The whole family was in attendance when, shortly after his birth, Cristofer was baptized at the Vatican. He, too, has been blessed with sensitivity for others. One day, I overheard him asking his mother to give him an extra sandwich for a child in his fifth-grade class because the other child did not have as much as others had. Probably because Cristofer came into our lives at a time when I was older, I have been able to be around his childhood a great deal. I love the fact that he is a voracious reader and an "old soul."

"It's not all playtime. Cristofer needs to fulfill his school responsibilities — even on plane trips."

I have seen him active and not a bit intimidated in a room full of adults (including presidential candidates and other political and civic leaders). I take pride in seeing him engaged in these one-on-one conversations, without Mom or Dad nearby. I especially like how well he relates to his siblings and looks up to them. Our favorite time together is riding around Little River Plantation and even hunting there.

Pilar de los Angeles Fernandez and her family Known to all as Pili or Tita, my sister can be described under a variety of headlines — great mother, super wife, the Mother Teresa of caring for animals, the ultimate photographer. The one exception is when I describe her as my older sister. (Possibly because she is two years younger than I.) Pili has been by my side from the day she was born, and lived through the emotionally unsettling experiences of our early days in Cuba and then New York City. I don't say it enough, but I love her a great deal. Her husband, Victor, adores her. Thus, I forgive him for not being Cuban. (Actually, he's a proud Argentinean.) Her sons, daughters-in-law and grandchildren love to be near Tita.

Carlos Padron An attorney and a dear friend for three decades, Carlos has been something of a daily companion. I chat with him almost every day on the way to work. We also chat when I get home. Constance jokes that he must have a spy camera at our house, since he mostly calls as we are about to begin dinner. He is a fantastic father to his five children and a devoted husband. As one would expect, our respective children are good friends. In many ways, I consider a day incomplete if Carlos and I haven't spoken at least once.

"My older sister, Pili and I. Actually, to tell the truth, she's two years younger than I am. But I do like to tease."

"At my son Alex's wedding: My sister Pilar (Pili) with her husband, Victor, and their two youngest children — Victor and Danny."

Cesar Alvarez:
*"A brilliant lawyer —
and I've never met
anyone with more
common sense. A
brother in almost ev-
ery sense of the word."*

Cesar Alvarez Ralph Waldo Emerson famously wrote, "I didn't find my friends; the good God gave them to me." That's how I feel about Cesar Alvarez. I've enjoyed having Cesar by my side for the last 35 years. He is the brother I never had. Our friendship has endured professional and business challenges as both of us experienced the ups and downs of life. In Cesar, I found the smartest person I ever met. What made him so smart was the gift of common sense. He also possesses the gift of humility and the gift of caring — even for those who did not know he was the wizard behind the screen who made it all happen. I owe much of what I have accomplished to Cesar and his guidance.

Dr. Roger Medel Roger is one of my few great friends, so much so that I could write a book dedicated only to him. We are different, but also alike in many ways. Through sheer determination, he developed into a terrific student, a pediatrician, a neonatologist and — as if that were not enough — he went back to school and received a master's degree in business administration.

"ROGER IS METHODICAL AND PATIENT. I LACK THESE QUALITIES, BUT I AM SLOWLY ACQUIRING THEM THANKS TO HIM."

As a businessman and a doctor, Roger started a neonatology group to treat very sick babies, often from the moment of birth. He grew the company into a $6 billion firm whose shares are traded through the New York Stock Exchange.

Roger is methodical and patient. I lack these qualities, but I am slowly acquiring them, largely because of him. His greatest quality, however, is his devotion to saving the lives of children. Also noteworthy is his devotion to medicine. He reinforces and validates my approach to business and to life: "Focus on others' well-being and good will come to you."

Roger is a husband, father, provider and protector. He is one of the greatest role models I have had. Even after 25 years, he remains a great teacher.

Peter Jimenez and his family
Peter and I go all the way back to 1989, and we trust each other completely. Among us, we kid that Peter is insecure about how much equity he owns. (It's a running joke.) His wife, Yamile, and the children are also good friends. Peter John, Victoria and Gabriel are as smart as their parents, both of whom hold multiple university degrees in industrial engineering, finance and healthcare. The family's passion: traveling to Tibet and other faraway lands.

Peter is a true friend — and he cares. A particularly likable fellow, Peter is a unifying force in the office. He has the ability to motivate people to go the extra mile, simply because he asks. That is a very special gift. Yamile is a "firecracker" who loves Peter and their family. They are an academically gifted unit driven to achieve excellence. At 15, Victoria went off to study German in Germany and, before long, she also had a job. Her brother Peter John attends Wake Forest University. And then there is Gabriel, a collector of exotic animals and a developing scientific researcher — at the age of 15! We love Peter and his family.

Jorge Rico and his family
I met Jorge in 1989 when I sold a fledgling company, CBAI, to the much larger Ramsay-HMO, at which Jorge worked fulltime as he also attended Saint Thomas University fulltime. Jorge is a special soul. I derive particular joy from my long relationship with Jorge, his wife, Isabel, and their three children. I always hear a sincere "I love you" from Danny, Jessie and Stephanie when we meet. Jorge is the kind of guy who is smart, likable and strategic with his thinking. But his best asset is his relationship with his family.

I have a special appreciation for Jorge, as he is anything but a "yes man." Jorge is true to his values and to his opinions. In most cases, he is right, which I eventually realize. He also is a well-rounded individual who can make the rest of us look like underachievers. Arriving home after a 15-hour day at the office, most of us would seek a quiet moment, but not this guy. If his children ask him to play touch football, he plays. Basketball? He plays. "Dad, I need help with math." He tutors. "Will you cook burgers?" He cooks. A superb person — that's Jorge.

Marcio Cabrera and his family
Again, Marcio, Peter, Jorge and I all met through the same company, Ramsay-HMO, after it acquired my company, CBAI. Marcio is not pleased when I call him a "recovering accountant." Consequently, I do it all the time to see how he is going to achieve his revenge. He is quick and lethal, and his sharp wit

Mike is much more than a business partner to me. He is mentor, friend, brother and simply an incredible example of someone who gives unconditionally of himself and of his wealth to our community.

Mike has taught me so many lessons. The most important of those is unselfishness and helping others. Mike's a rescuer. He gives his time, shares his experiences, provides guidance and contributes resources (mostly without being asked).

As a busy executive, his approach is relentless. When Mike believes in something, he will pursue it until he accomplishes the goal. He feeds on succeeding when everyone else tells him that success is not possible. Mike is deeply insightful, understands people and understands that great people make great companies. He won't hesitate to replace those who are mediocre. At the same time, he's also very loyal to people who are loyal to him — and who perform.

Mike's passion is selling. With selling comes convincing. He starts, buys, builds and sells companies. He does not become enamored with any company he owns. Instead he is focused on the end game — buy low and sell high, but always sell. Many entrepreneurs start their own businesses and build them for their families. Mike builds businesses and sells them for his family.

He's a great listener. He collaborates with those he trusts, but always pursues what he believes in (regardless of what those around him might think). His success is driven by that relentless spirit to disregard the naysayers. If someone gets in the way of achieving Mike's objective, he will work with, through or around that person until he or she either gives up or gives in — and Mike's goal is accomplished.

As a partner, Mike can be tough, but he always is fair. He respects your opinion and your view. He's always there for you, especially if you are in need.

I am so fortunate to be his partner — and his friend.

Jorge Rico
BUSINESS PARTNER

Chapter 9

I have climbed mountains and crossed valleys, and I have walked longer in a day than I ever thought I was capable of lasting.

The Meseta: "Another village, another day being punished by the sun."

always surprises me. Miriam and the children — Katrina, Adrian and Gabriel (Gabo) — also are close to our family.

It's easy to read Marcio. He wears his feelings on his face — relaxed, happy, upset or stressed. All he has to do is walk into a room and you know his mood before he opens his mouth. I remember one time when his daughter, Katrina, surprised him by arriving at the office after a flight from Boston, dropping in to see her dad. His first reaction was a flood of tears — tears of joy. He talks often about how he met Miriam and how much she means to him. And about how much he admires Adrian's character and quietness. And then there is Gabriel — the mini Marcio.

Marcio has demonstrated a magnitude of loyalty that's hard to find in today's society. We disagree often, but we always hug and I know that we would do whatever was needed for each other. Lastly . . . his laughter. He always can be located and identified merely through his unique laugh. It brightens the largest room.

Luis Gonzalez and his family

Luis is the latest addition to our group, as we met in 2006. He joined us shortly after the rest of us stepped out of operations and into investing. Luis probes into details of the deals, and he manages our relationships with banks and law firms. His wife, Monica, and son, Phillip, as the saying goes, complete him. I look forward to our future years together.

For years, our five families have grown closer. In fact, we treat each other more as relatives than as business associates. We enjoy having the families together for Thanksgiving at our Little River Plantation near Tallahassee. I'm sure that Little River's manager, Key Barnes, wonders each year how our Cuban families interact, and it's always a great time for us. I know that we unintentionally place some stress on Key, but we love him and his dog, Lucy.

Dr. Barbara Cowley

Barbara and I have worked together for two decades. She has led the medical departments at many of our companies, and she has done so with a great deal of success. Some people misjudge her because of her sweet disposition and quiet demeanor, but she is a force with which to be reckoned. If we need medical advice, she always is near.

Barbara and her husband, Andres, are great friends. Though she can be sedate, he often is the life of a party. A successful gastroenterologist, Andres cannot be overlooked when he is in a room — or even a baseball stadium.

Carlos Fernandez Carlito Fernandez is like family to us. We met decades ago when he was working for a competitor. Before long, he joined one of our firms. I often joke that, when I met him, he worked at a car wash, which obviously is not true. He, his wife, Ysney, and their children form a terrific family. I've been honored to watch as he developed into a professional and successful executive, but it is his unquestionable loyalty that truly distinguishes him.

Tomas Orozco Tomas, Ivette and their family are part of our inner circle of friends. He is smart, cunning and very funny. I would also add "creatively unorthodox." The first year Tomas worked with one of our companies, I soon learned about how he manages to get his way. As I walked passed his office, I noticed a young man behind a desk, feet propped up on a credenza, one arm folded behind his head as he spoke on the phone. What I heard stopped me in my tracks. With a great deal of authority, Tomas was barking demands. "Listen," he said, "I will not wait for this report past the end of the day! I want you to drop whatever you are doing and jump on this now! I really don't care if you have to skip lunch and dinner but I want that report!"

I was shocked because, although I had met him only a couple of times before in group situations, he had managed to imitate my voice perfectly! He was highly effective in making people jump when he called — as they thought they were talking to me. I could not help but laugh at his ingenuity, and soon had him promoted.

Tomas is a go-to guy when we need results. He is creative, unorthodox and results-oriented. During more than 20 years of working together, Tomas has grown from an effective impersonator to a seasoned executive.

Lourdes Martin I refer to her as my second boss (after my wife, Constance). In fact, second only to Constance, Lourdes makes my life possible. She is unflappable and always pleasant to the ultimate degree. I have a friend who jokingly tells me that Lourdes is so calm that she should be working with suicide patients or as a psychologist. All kidding aside, there is no one like Lourdes. I am blessed to "work for her."

OCTOBER 11

Morning, Mansilla de las Mulas

Dear friends, may God be with you as He guides your path in life. It is a pleasure to have this opportunity to write to you and share this journey, now in its third week. I can tell you that it has been more wonderful and challenging than expected — much like life itself.

I have climbed mountains and crossed valleys, and I have walked longer in a day than I ever thought I was capable of lasting. They say that, in this part of northern Spain, there are only two seasons: winter and summer, and winter comes across like a lion.

During the last few days, I have started my hike at 4 or 5 a.m. in order to pick up some time. With a small head lantern, I was able to find the yellow arrows that mark the entire 508-mile path. But by midday, the roaring cold wind would cut through my clothing as if I were naked. At one point, I learned how to tie up a few pairs of socks and form a long scarf that was very helpful.

Still, I have developed a bad cold. For now, I have checked into a small inn to recover. Soon, I will move on to beautiful León to meet my friend John Raslowsky II, current president of the school I attended as a teenager in New York City, Xavier High School, at the beautiful Hostal de San Marcos. I will be glad that one of Xavier's sons, whom I and most people call Jack, will be with me for a few days.

My pilgrimage for ill children everywhere will continue for another two or three weeks, as I work to bring attention to their needs and challenges.

The statue of an El Camino pilgrim in the city of León. "I'm halfway to the end — and still smiling."

OCTOBER 11
En route to León

In the year 1154, they began building the structure now known as the Hostal de San Marcos within the walled city of León. A 16th-century gem, it was intended to provide aid and healthcare to pilgrims and children traveling with them as they made their way to Santiago de Compostela, my destination. As the economy changed over time, the hospital and boarding services closed. Later, it became a prison that many called a concentration camp during the Spanish Civil War.

There is a lesson here: Those of us who do not know history are likely to repeat it.

In our country, we are in a massive paradigm shift involving healthcare. It is up to us to make sure that institutions such as hospitals that specialize in caring for ill children continue to provide high-quality services.

As I have traveled more than 300 miles during the last three weeks, I have yet to see one hospital that is dedicated to children. All local children in severe need must be transported hundreds of miles in order to receive care. This could happen to us some day, but today you can help by supporting our cause. Please consider history, and most importantly please consider our future and our children. Please support this mission, and please be generous.

Burbling fountains in the main plaza of León — "and a good place to soak your feet." Alongside is the scallop shell representing El Camino — here in bronze and embedded in the cobblestones.

CHAPTER **TEN**

RELATIONSHIPS AND NETWORKING — KEYS TO SUCCESS

"The tiniest seed can produce a redwood — or even save a life."

During my life, I've had the opportunity (as have you) to meet thousands of people. I never regretted meeting a single one of them. Each person is a door that needs to be opened — and what you see beyond the threshold may change your life, usually for the better. In many cases, these encounters have changed mine.

As my father used to say when referring to business, "There are opportunities all around us. All we have to do is take action." In the end, this statement is not as much about business as it is about people.

Had it not been for Eugenio, the man at the airport fence in Mexico City, I may not have heard the whisper of the words, "You have to take care of those who come after you."

Had I not introduced myself to a man named Arnold Grossman in the lobby of a building waiting for the rain to stop, I may not have started my first business. Arnold turned out to be the owner of that building. One thing led to another, and he later became my first investor and an always-reliable friend and financial supporter.

Had I not hijacked a conversation and asked a woman at the table, "Are you married?" I may never have met Constance, the person who changed my life and became my wife.

Never forget that the person who may become pivotal in your life could be anywhere: On an elevator. Sitting next to you in class. Someone who contacts you through a mutual friend. Let me share two true stories that illustrate the importance of relationships and networking — and that also illustrate two other points: 1. You never can predict the full future impact or value of a single, simple act; and 2. Developing strong relationships has been a crucial key to my success and can prove vitally important in what matters most — protecting and even preserving the lives of those we love.

True Story No. 1: Rafael Kravec

One of my dearest and best friends is Rafael Kravec, born in Holguin, Cuba, to Jewish parents who had fled the madness of Nazism to the relative safety of Cuba.

Raised in a poor, ghetto-like neighborhood in Havana, Rafael made his way to Miami, where he first sold flowers for an importer, then worked at the Burdines department store, and ultimately earned his fortune as founder and chief executive officer of French Fragrances, a large and publicly traded company.

Rafael stepped down as CEO of French Fragrances in 1998, after his company was acquired by Elizabeth Arden. That freed him to devote more time to another passion: the preservation and security of Israel.

I love Rafael. The brotherhood that I feel for this man is a brotherhood I feel for few others. What's unique about him and what I admire so much about him is this: He's a self-made man, extremely humble and with an incredible desire to help others, especially those in Israel.

Now, largely because of Rafael, I share this passion. I am not Jewish, but I relate on many levels to Jewish people and to Israelis. I believe that Israel must survive and prosper, not only as a haven for the world's Jewish people but as an example of what dedicated people can achieve when they work toward a common objective.

Consequently, I have become an active supporter of Israeli projects and causes, both financially and in spirit, and this all began with Rafael.

For years, as he traveled around the world on business, Rafael quietly assisted

Israeli diplomats and others by carrying messages and information between them and people in foreign countries. Rafael also had a childhood relationship with Shimon Peres, a relationship that deepened through the years, as Peres served Israel in a variety of ways. A former prime minister, a genuine elder statesman of Israel, Peres also completed a seven-year term as that nation's president.

Rafael doesn't brag or even talk very much about his work on behalf of Israel, but one day many years ago, he told me that Peres was coming to South Florida and that I should meet this prominent Israeli.

So, we met, and Peres told me about a project he was launching to help Palestinian children and, in a real way, their Palestinian parents. Clearly, anything that bound Palestinians a little tighter to Israel had to be good, so I offered to help financially or in any other way to support the project.

This was the first of a series of such episodes, so many that at one point, during a visit to Israel, I was publicly hailed as "a key non-Jewish contributor" to that country.

"My good friend Rafael Kravec is one of my great mentors and friends. I've learned so much from him."

Chris and Pat Riley: "Two of the finest people I've ever known. He is the epitome of a visionary."

I was a little embarrassed by the attention, but I must admit that it was nice to be recognized by the Israeli leadership.

Over the years and during many trips to Israel, my family and I have been treated extremely well by the fine people of that nation. We have traveled in unusual circumstances as we met some of the nation's most prominent leaders and citizens.

Helping Israel and its people survive and thrive matters to me.

I also came to know quite well a high-ranking member of Israel's intelligence agency, the Shin Bet. He remains, to this day, a close friend. I shall call him Shlomi.

Shlomi and I have done each a few favors, including one that turned out to be quite amusing.

In 2013, the Miami Heat basketball team was in its final playoff series for another NBA championship. As it happened, Shlomi was in Washington, D.C., with his wife. He was briefing U.S. intelligence officials about terrorist activities in the Middle East and Europe.

The day before the final game, he called me because he knew that I had Heat season tickets and he wanted to experience the excitement associated with any championship game. Unfortunately, I had given my seats to my children. But, just as I was in Shlomi's network of friends, Heat President Pat Riley was in my network of friends.

In fact, Pat and his wife, Chris, are dear personal friends. Pat was one of the world's greatest basketball coaches, and he is a business leader and a mentor to many. Those who don't know him and see him from afar may think that they are seeing a stone-faced, unemotional man, but they are so very wrong. Often, someone will ask me, "Is he nice?" "Nice" would be an understatement. Pat is a class act to the core, and Chris is a true delight.

What makes Pat so special is that he cares about his players and all of those around him. He is unselfish. He is a true visionary and an incredible storyteller. Those are some of the attributes that make him one of the greatest motivators I ever have known. Like all self-made people I have met, Pat starts with honesty and an intimate knowledge of the individuals or the organizations with whom he is dealing. He is also demanding and does not settle for anything but full commitment.

So, Pat responded promptly to my request for tickets, and soon my Israeli friends were on a flight from Washington to Miami. Pat generously gave us four prime seats — two for my friends and two for Constance and me. The game was terrific. The Heat won. It was a perfect night.

But . . . I should have known not to take anything for granted. The next morning, prominently displayed on the front page of the *Miami Herald* was a picture of Heat star (and also a close friend) Ray Allen taking the winning shot and, in the background, one could easily see Shlomi, a man who only lives in the shadows.

The following day, Shlomi called me and said, with a chuckle, that he received many calls from associates in the intelligence community who jokingly shared with him that his cover had been blown.

So, anyway, this relationship proved particularly valuable when my daughter, Michelle, decided to spend a month in a small village of South Africa, working at an animal rehabilitation center. I told her that I was concerned. This was not a secure area; her plane had to land in the middle of nowhere, and I just didn't feel good about any of this.

"LOOK, THIS IS HOW DANGEROUS IT IS THERE. YOU CANNOT GO OFF THE RESERVATION ... DON'T DO ANYTHING STUPID."

At about this time, Shlomi was in Washington again. I called him and told him about my concerns. So, he flew to Miami, met with Michelle and told her, "Look, this is how dangerous it is there. You cannot go off the reservation to go into town and so on. Just don't do anything stupid."

He also told her to wear a blue scarf and a baseball cap when she came out of the airplane in Johannesburg. You can guess the rest: He had one or more Israeli agents keeping an eye on her the entire time she was in South Africa.

One day, Shlomi called me and said, "So, things are fine, but you might want to call Michelle because she went off the reservation, and she's on the beach right now."

You can bet that I made that call. The point is this:

I couldn't possibly know that — because I helped a friend from Israel so many years ago and nurtured other strong relationships with Israelis — an Israeli would be in a position to keep my daughter safe.

But that's what happened, and what could be more important than that?

Daughter Michelle at a South African animal rehabilitation camp giving an antibiotic to a young kudu.

True Story No. 2: My Grandfather and the Sandwiches

Many years ago, when my immediate family was still in Cuba, it was difficult to support either side in the brewing revolution.

For some, Fidel Castro seemed like a liberator, but we now know what he really was and is — a dictator who has impoverished the nation and condemned its citizens to hardship for more than 50 years. At the same time, however, Cuban dictator Fulgencio Batista maintained control over the country, and he was supported by many thugs, including a senator, Rolando Masferrer, founder of Los Tigres de Masferrer, a ruthless guerrilla group that led a reign of terror in our part of Cuba. They were criminals and bullies, and they made friends with no one of decency.

Still, it was smart to try to stay on the good side of these people. At some point, Masferrer visited one of my father's sandwich shops and my father refused to take payment. "No, it's on me," my father said. "For you and for your guys."

Alas, one day after that, my paternal grandfather and a young associate, who at the time supported Castro, were on their way to make deliveries to sugar mills in the mountains, and they decided also to deliver supplies to Castro's people, who were in the area.

Unfortunately, they got caught by some of Masferrer's men and were taken to a secluded house for interrogation. These people sent my father a note, demanding $5,000 or my grandfather would be killed. At this point, they were not just common kidnappers. They also had a reputation of torturing and murdering their captives.

My father got on a plane to Havana, went to Masferrer's office and pleaded his case. Masferrer said, "You know, your father shouldn't have been doing that. It's treason, but because you were polite to me, I will make sure your father is let go. But somebody has to pay the price."

That somebody was my grandfather's young associate, who was executed as my grandfather watched. Then, my grandfather was freed.

So, there you have it. A simple relationship, formed over an inexpensive sandwich between a monstrous man and my wonderful father, ended up saving the life of my grandfather.

When it comes to networking and developing relationships, even the tiniest seed can produce a redwood or even save a life.

Grandfather Miguel Fernandez Rojas and his wife Mariana Escancell, dressed in clothing rented for the occasion (circa 1920). He was the son of Spaniards. "I can remember his big blue eyes. I don't remember her; they divorced when my father was quite young."

OCTOBER 11–12

León, Correspondence with my friend, David Lawrence Jr.

To Dave Lawrence: My friend, here is a challenge. While walking in the Basque country, I read an article about a girl who needs cardiac surgery. The whole region is consumed in collecting bottle tops to sell them and pay for her surgery. I may be able to help. Can you find the contact info of the reporter? I will be in León for a few days resting from a bad cold.

From Dave Lawrence: Most of the coverage goes back many months. I see stories from EFE, the Spanish news agency; a newspaper called Noticias de Navarra (with no reporter's byline); and from ABC, a newspaper based in Madrid. [Phone numbers are provided.] So far as I can tell, it is not a heart problem but rather a chromosome problem, which means the young girl cannot eat or drink through her mouth, but instead gets food and water through some sort of gastric probe. Supposedly, there are only four such cases in the world. Collections have been made through two Spanish banks. I hope this helps. Let me know how else I might help.

To Dave Lawrence: You understood the story better than I did. I have been under the weather with this bad cold, staying in a small town, and my reading glasses are nowhere to be found. I will try to reach the paper and ask questions. . . .

I am getting better. I expect that by tomorrow, I can hit the road, though I'll be slower. But here is my problem: I get sidetracked easily by the people I meet. The German who carried a small Bible and learned multiple languages so he could attend Mass at every church along the way. He was not a "nut case." He was a devoted soul. Or the family that has a rented car so they could provide taxi services and try to support themselves. (They own that car now.)

I can go on. There are so many people in real need and it bothers me that we, in the United States, have so many opportunities and so often squander them. Desire, drive, intensity and the ability to fall and get up — that trumps IQ any day.

I have been humbled by this journey.

OCTOBER 12

An extra day of rest in León

We are now past the halfway point of our trip and I am happy to share with you some events that have occurred and that I view as significant — maybe not significant from the perspective of life-changing events, but significant from a personal perspective, as they bring me to the core of who I am.

There was an incident a few days ago (it seems like weeks ago) in which a taxi driver drove me from a certain location to a nonscheduled stop in my route — a location that was significant from a historical point of view. This individual, whom I had never met before, told me that the taxi (really just a personal car that is rented for use as a taxi) did not belong to her. It belonged to someone else who rented it to her.

The driver was a woman of low income, living in a very small town in the middle of nowhere, but her personal story was interesting. Her grandfather or great-grandfather had moved to Cuba in the early 1900s, made it his home and married a Cuban woman. He then returned to Spain with what at that time must have seemed a large sum of money, but his descendants had spent it all.

Upon our return, I asked her if she would introduce me to the man who owned the car. I had a conversation with that man, the car owner, and today the taxi driver is the owner of that automobile. This woman was in shock that someone, a stranger, would do something of such magnitude for her and expect nothing in return. As she dropped me off, she cried and she said, "I have always believed in angels, but I never met one before."

The investment was quite small. I spent less than $2,000, but hopefully this event will change this woman's life, or at least show her that someone cares for her.

There have been many events that have occurred during the last three weeks on this road, El Camino, that I cannot explain. But I do believe that my life is changing for the better as a result of this experience.

May tomorrow, Sunday, be a day of rest and reflection for us.

Mid-October 2013: "I'm in the Spanish region of Castilla and León in the company of two compatriots during my walk: Stephen, the Scottish writer, and Nuria, a nurse from Madrid."

OCTOBER 13–15

León to Astorga

During these days, I did not write and send any updates, as Jack Raslowsky of Xavier High School, who met me in León, and I walked our paths and allowed our souls to engage. I had not seen Jack in years. He was following my El Camino journey on Facebook, and before I knew it, he said, "I'll be there." His companionship had not been in my plans, but I am so glad that he joined me.

I still don't know exactly how it happened. Somehow, Jack heard about my walk. He sent me a note, wishing me the best. Before I knew it, I invited him to join me, and he accepted. Now, we are together.

I felt blessed to have him at my side. His presence provided an even greater sense of spirituality. At one time, Jack had contemplated becoming a Jesuit priest and, although he has taken another path, he carried himself in a spiritual fashion. Full of knowledge and generosity, he provided me with a new connection and deep sense of tranquility. Also, not to be overlooked, he brought along a lively sense of humor.

We shared stories about our upbringings and about particularly defining periods of our lives. He spoke a great deal about his deep faith in God, and I benefited from his words.

Meanwhile, onward we go. The weather clearly has changed from the days in the Pyrenees. It is much cooler, and it rains intermittently.

OCTOBER 16

Astorga

I am five days away from it being one month since I left for El Camino. Originally, I projected that I would be close to the finish line by now, but it wasn't meant to be, as I have faced setbacks. Sometimes, the children in the hospital and under medical care face their own setbacks, but theirs are much more serious.

As a result of a bad cold and steady rain, my progress has been slowed. Walking in red clay mud is like walking on glue. Yesterday was a particularly bad day. We should have completed our task in seven to eight hours, but it took more than 12 hours in the rain and with other challenges.

The good news is that, after half a day on the road, I had a comfortable bed to crash on. On the other hand, children in need have to face issues that take longer than 12 hours to resolve. They need our support, and I ask you to help us by contributing all that you can.

CHAPTER**ELEVEN**

EL CAMINO DE SANTIAGO —
THE PILGRIMAGE

"I have been humbled by this journey. My life is changing for the better. I am in love with the experience."

Let us now return to the event that serves as both the stimulus for and the framework of this book — the 508-mile trek through southernmost France and northern Spain known as El Camino de Santiago.

Why in the world would a 61-year-old corporate chairman and CEO with a bad back, weak ankles, two previous heart attacks, a recent recovery from prostate cancer surgery, no previous experience with long hikes and no profound religious beliefs begin and complete the arduous Christian pilgrimage also known as the Way of Saint James? (In case you're wondering, we did the calculation: Hiking 508 miles requires about 3 million steps.)

How did I become a pilgrim, in Spanish *peregrino*, in Italian *pellegrino*? To this day, I'm not entirely certain of the answer. Let's see if we can figure it out together.

In some ways, the challenge began two years earlier when, out of the blue, a dear and beloved friend, Aileen Ugalde, sent me a photo and she wrote, "I'm doing El Camino in Spain and I'm having a wonderful time." I was thrilled for her, but I had no idea what she was talking about. To be honest, I had never heard of El Camino, but I looked it up and thought, *Well, that's interesting, but I'm not an exercise guy. I'm old. I'd never do this.*

Fast forward a couple of years. My daughter, Michelle, who is a student at the University of Miami, suddenly says that she would like to walk along part of that route. I have four sons and just one daughter, so of course I do anything she wants me to do. Michelle is much more religious than I am, and she and I sometimes take vacations together, so I said, "Okay, you make the arrangements. I'll just go along for the walk." She soon had lunch with our good friend Aileen, who was the University of Miami's general counsel, and at home Michelle was more excited than ever.

"I WAS JUST ALONG FOR THE RIDE, BUT IT WAS ONE OF THE MOST FANTASTIC EXPERIENCES I EVER HAD."

And, so, we did it. I was just along for the ride, but it was one of the most fantastic experiences I ever had. Nine days moving east to west, from Sarria to Santiago de Compostela, typically considered the terminal point of El Camino, a city in the Galicia region of northwestern Spain built largely around a gorgeous cathedral and shrine to Saint James the Great. Those nine days with my daughter seemed magical.

Now, we're back in Florida and, as I mentioned, my granddaughter Daniella is in the children's hospital for heart surgery. In the waiting room, I meet that mother of an adopted child also undergoing surgery, and the mother has that frightened, desperate look in her eyes. Suddenly, it all just fell into place.

I told my friends at the hospital, "I'm going to do this pilgrimage, and I'm going to do this to raise money for people like that mother." It was not about funding a new

"This picture was an early inspiration for my embarking on this great journey. My friend Aileen Ugalde suggested it, having just taken El Camino herself with her daughter Gabriela (shown here)."

Cesar Alvarez: "He looked pretty sharp on arrival (look at his fancy shoes!). But his heart is in the right place."

building or about pumping up the general fund. It was specifically about financial assistance for needy patients and their families.

Anyway, I began training and planning and otherwise preparing for the walk, and we began spreading the word through email, a website and social media outlets such as Facebook. The response was immediate and heartwarming.

On Friday, August 16, 2013, we distributed the first email about my plan to raise $1 million through the walk. Four days later, we already had nearly $500,000 in confirmed donations and a significant additional amount in pledges. Four days — more than a half-million dollars. I hardly could believe it.

The response was so terrific that, within a few weeks, we happily elevated the goal. Now, the objective was to raise $3 million — one dollar for every step required to complete El Camino. Again, this was a 508-mile trek from Saint-Jean-Pied-de-Port to Santiago de Compostela. Forty to 50 days through mountains, farmland, ancient rural hamlets, forests and rivers.

"FOR THE FIRST TIME, I WAS NOT LIVING FOR TOMORROW OR IN RESPONSE TO YESTERDAY; I WAS LIVING IN THE MOMENT."

WALKING IN ANCIENT FOOTSTEPS

This was something I really wanted to do myself. I felt that I needed some time and space to get away from the everyday pressures of life, to ponder who I was and where I was along this journey through life. But my good and great friend Cesar Alvarez, whom I met almost 40 years ago when I was a lowly insurance agent and who, as I mentioned, now is co-chairman of Greenberg Traurig, the international law firm, insisted on joining me for the first week.

El Camino is truly ancient, a path followed by millions of people since the ninth century. It carries pilgrims across southern France and northern Spain to Santiago de Compostela. *Santiago* is a local Galician evolution of "Saint James." *Compostela* derives from Latin for "field of the star." Here it is said that Saint James, the patron saint of Spain, is buried under the city's cathedral.

The route is full of messages that you learn to read along the way, and the journey is one that swiftly connects itself to your internal being, to your soul. With each step I took and with each day that passed, I became more absorbed by the experience and the adventure. For the first time, I was not living for tomorrow or in response to yesterday; I was living in the moment.

Each step I took touched the invisible footprints of millions of other travelers who had taken this quiet, dusty, shaded and at times moss-covered path — a path followed by not only the devout but also by Roman legions and invading armies that left their marks along the way.

As you sit just off the road, gazing at the surroundings, your mind wanders. You almost can hear the voices, the marching feet, the clashing of swords. You almost can hear the whispers of a medieval family trying not to attract the attention of thieves or other forms of ill fortune. All of them bound for the same destination — Santiago de Compostela and the shrine of Saint James.

"Jack Raslowsky and me: We met years before at Xavier High, and then became great friends on El Camino."

"Were not our hearts on fire as he talked to us on the road and explained the scriptures to us? They set out that instant and returned to Jerusalem. There they found the Eleven assembled together with their companions who said to them, 'The Lord has indeed risen and appeared to Simon.' Then they told them the story of what had happened on the road and how they recognized him in the breaking of the bread." — Luke 24:32–35

So ends Luke's story of Cleopas and his companion walking the road to Emmaus. There is no more apt metaphor for my journey on the Camino this fall with Mike Fernandez '72 than the Emmaus story.

I joined Mike in León, Spain, weeks into his pilgrimage. His invitation to join him was a generous surprise. From our first conversation walking the grounds of the Hostal de San Marcos — once a hospital for pilgrims and then a prison during the Spanish Civil War — it was clear God was with us.

Much of the week it was just Mike and me, walking for hours on a trail that millions before us have taken since the ninth century. The time together was a great gift: a gift of stories about New York and Cuba, Hoboken and Miami; about our mothers and fathers; about children and family; about Jesuits and the Church; about work and leisure, faith and doubt, lessons learned, gifts and talents.

We spoke, too, about the ill children Mike has met through his work with a children's hospital. He carried a set of cards with the pictures, names and backgrounds of dozens of sick children. He would pray for particular children each day. Though he carried those cards in his backpack, he carried the kids in his heart. As I often said to Mike, there are many ways to do the Camino. I began the journey not knowing what to expect. I was excited to get to know Mike better, to be on pilgrimage, to walk the road with other pilgrims. What I experienced was a gift. And like all gifts of the spirit, I will always carry it with me.

Walter Brueggemann describes good fellowship as "serious conversation leading to blessed communion." In the walking, questioning and eating together, my heart was on fire. Like Cleopas who encountered the living God on the walk to Emmaus, we encountered Him on the walk to Santiago de Compostela. And in our stepping away, I was reminded that God walks with us not only on the Camino, but wherever the journey takes us. It is a gift for which I am deeply grateful.

Jack Raslowsky

PRESIDENT, XAVIER HIGH SCHOOL

OCTOBER 17–18

Astorga to La Cruz de Ferro

During the past few days, I have gotten to know Jack well and hopefully he has gotten to know me. We have much in common. For two guys who barely knew each other a week earlier, we have now connected on many levels.

We spoke mostly about our families and, in particular, our children. I learned a great deal about Jack, his deep faith and his commitment to the students he leads. Physically, he is much stronger than I am; he was looking forward to running the New York City Marathon upon his return in a few days. I also learned about the Jesuit order in more detail than ever.

I am *involved* in my spiritual journey, but Jack is *committed*. I admire his clarity of life. At one point, our trail passed a long series of handmade crosses left behind by previous pilgrims. This display extended for more than a mile. It was profoundly moving.

It was somewhere along the road that I saw just ahead of us a figure that I was familiar with. At a distance I could recognize him by his shape, pants, hat and backpack. It was Stephen, the writer from Scotland.

Soon, we caught up to him, and I introduced my friend from El Camino, Stephen, to my friend from my old high school, Jack. We would walk together for the next day.

A few hours later, the three of us were getting close to where our trail intercepted another that led to a small town about 100 yards north. At the intersection, we met a man in his 80s, who was happy to speak with us. He said he stands by the trail every day, waiting for pilgrims to walk by, hoping they are willing to chat.

"Stephen, the Scotsman, and I speak to Bienvenido (a name meaning 'welcome'). Maybe 20 years older than I, he looked much younger. He was a well-informed man, simply by listening to the stories of so many pilgrims. Below: The "yellow arrow" pin found all along El Camino, giving direction to travelers."

He told us about his life during the Spanish Civil War. His dad left to fight in the war and never returned. Then just a child, he and his young brother, both under 10 years old, stayed with their mother and were considered the men of the house. Their only food came from what they could grow in the fields or could hunt in the nearby forest. When strangers or soldiers came, the boys' job was to take the flock of sheep into the woods and protect it until their mother came for them.

He pointed at our rain gear and said, "We did not have waterproof clothing, and when it rained and we had to stay overnight in the woods, those were very long nights." It was a fascinating chat, but we had to move on, so we did.

Somewhere between the villages of Foncebadón and Manjarín, we walked, single file, up a rocky mountain trail. It was cold, windy and wet. It felt as if we were walking in the clouds.

Our destination was La Cruz de Ferro, "the Iron Cross," a historical point on El Camino and one of my two principal destinations during this journey. It is a monument along El Camino where many people deposit rocks, stones or other items that they've carried from home.

Ahead of us, we could see a person who would fade in and out of sight in the rolling fog and mist. This person had a fluorescent green backpack cover. With every step, we would get a bit closer. After a while, we were just a few steps behind this person and recognized that it was a tall woman, carrying a very large backpack.

As we passed her, we wished her *buen camino*, and as she turned her face to wish us the same, we could not help but notice that she did not seem well. We offered to help her with her backpack, and the tall

German woman, in her 40s, gratefully accepted. A few hours later, the three of us arrived at the Iron Cross.

This is the only time during the hike that my emotions overtook me. Jack offered to film me as I stood in front of La Cruz and read aloud the names of each child given to me by the children's hospital, as I placed each card and picture beside the Cruz.

This is what Jack later wrote about that moment:

"When we left those cards at the Iron Cross, we commended those kids to the prayer of all the pilgrims who came before and would come after. Saint Ignatius [Saint James] reminds us of God's presence in our deepest desires. Mike's desires for those children — desires for wholeness and healing, desires for life lived in abundance — were indeed holy desires."

Because God placed Jack by my side, I always will remember this moment and that I was able to capture the images.

The Iron Cross: "It was here that I placed pictures of each child at the hospital. I stood on a pile of what must be millions of stones brought here by pilgrims. Each stone represents a prayer — and gratitude."

The Templar Castle in Ponferrada, Spain, built in the 12th century and housing a magnificent library of Templar Knights writings and history and copies of works by Leonardo da Vinci.

As my father used to say when referring to business, "There are opportunities all around us. All we have to do is take action."

OCTOBER 19

Ponferrada

Today, I arrived at Ponferrada and my road friend, Jack Raslowsky, headed back to New York City.

It's interesting how one keeps encountering people who one has met along El Camino, and in this case, how one can earn a reaffirmation of this great life.

Today, we once again saw the German woman in her 40s, the woman with the green backpack cover. It turns out that she is terminally ill. Today, all she said was: "Yesterday, I left my broken heart at the Iron Cross." She did not look well, and just as soon as she arrived, she was on her way again. I hope to see her again.

This has been a journey that has required more than physical strength. Most of the challenge has been "mind over matter," knowing that, at any point, I could have quit. It was a daily temptation and one that could have been easily based on the weather, the extreme heat and then the extreme cold, the thick mist through most of the mountains where one could barely see 50 feet ahead, the windy days, and these darned, small, hand-posted signs tacked on fences and trees, offering taxi services to the nearest city.

But it would have been embarrassing to quit in light of the two missions I had: The first, to visit the sanctuary at Loyola, where I had committed to deliver a crucifix given to me by my dear Jesuit leader who passed away. The second was a personal goal to reach the Iron Cross, where I read the names of sick children.

Thank God, I was able to do both — and more.

"At the base of the Iron Cross, I placed the laminated picture of each child from the children's hospital. It was the only time I cried."

CHAPTER**TWELVE**

THE GIFT OF TODAY — A GIFT TO BE USED WISELY

"We have a profound responsibility to each other."

During that preliminary segment of El Camino in May, my daughter Michelle shared an interesting insight and then an interesting question.

The route is filled with hills. You go up a hill, and down a hill. Up a hill and down a hill. Over and over. She said, "I thought that going up the hill was the hardest part, but then I realized that going down the hill was the hardest because it hurt my knees."

There was a brief pause, and I asked her, "Do you have a question?"

"Yes," she replied. "So, why do you keep building your own hills, your businesses, this walk, these challenges? You certainly don't need to work, and every time you sell something, you jump back in with something else."

I thought that was a pretty good question, and it took a while to construct but I gave her this answer:

One reason is the fear — fear of being poor again. It's probably the same thing that people coming out of the Holocaust felt. I have read that, because of the experiences they endured, they always felt a level of insecurity, no matter how wealthy some may have become.

The other reason is validation — the feeling that I'm worth something. I'm good at something. Because I never made it through college, I always had a chip on my shoulder about that. That's the bottom line for me: fear and validation.

I said, "Have you noticed what happens when I sell a company?" She said, "No. You must be happy." And I said, "No, I get very depressed. Because I don't know what's going to come next. I have to reinvent myself somehow, do something else."

In some ways, as I get older, it's becoming more difficult and more challenging.

"I LOVED CUBA BECAUSE IT WAS MY PAST. I LOVE THE UNITED STATES BECAUSE IT IS MY FUTURE AND THAT OF MY FAMILY."

I want to help people and I also believe in the power of one's imagination, of "visualization," the power of seeing your goals to the point where you can make them materialize. I believe in the power of the individual.

When it comes to business and life, sometimes our elected leaders act as if we are incapable of taking care of ourselves, as if we need to be protected from our own acts. Don't take me wrong — there is a need for government and there is a need for laws, but I am concerned about the growth of ever-increasing governmental power and the growing dependency of some people on government.

I come from a country, Cuba, where the government tells you how to do everything, and that certainly doesn't work.

Before I went back to Cuba for a visit in 1999, I read two or three books written by Cuban Americans about their experiences in going back for the first time. Maybe I became desensitized after reading about how emotional it was for them, but when I went to Cuba, the experience did not move me as much as it concerned me. It was not even emotional to see my old house there. It was just matter of fact. "I'm here. I used to live here. Big deal."

Mike's journey on El Camino gave him genuine nourishment for the soul. He strengthened his muscles; more importantly, he strengthened his faith and spirit.

Mike is my cherished friend. As impressive as he is as a businessman, he's even more impressive in his love for family and friends, and his passion for people and community.

Mike's a shining example of a servant-leader, a person dedicated to the growth and well-being of people and their communities. How blessed we are for his commitment and contributions to the greater good of a Greater Miami.

Eduardo J. Padrón

PRESIDENT OF MIAMI DADE COLLEGE

But I saw how, in a matter of decades, the power of big government could destroy a nation and its people. How it could suppress the ability to dream and to become risk-takers. Through its policies, big government had created a climate in which risk-taking was punishable; therefore, few people took risks. Those who did take risks and found themselves outside the guidelines dictated by policy paid a high price — sometimes even forfeiting their freedom.

I loved Cuba because it was my past. I love the United States of America because it is my future and it is the future of my family. That does not mean that I do not care

No one in sight. *"I am truly pleased that I took this journey when there were so few on the trail. Here you see young vineyards in the making."*

Each day is unique. We will never experience this day again. Today is a gift. Let's use it wisely – and with generosity.

"*I have always loved the sea. In 1999, when I returned to Cuba for the first time since leaving in 1964, I met Ernest Hemingway's boat captain. I found Gregorio Fuentes living in a small home with his son. He was born in the Canary Islands off the coast of northern Afrrica. His hands were twice as large as mine – and seemed as rough as a shark's skin.*"

232

about what happens in my country of birth and to its people. I will, as I have been doing for decades, continue to help the people of my native land work toward a free and democratic society.

After my very first trip overseas, when I came back to the United States, I was home. The United States allowed me to become the person I am today.

Embrace the Risk Takers

I am not bullheaded about politics; I try to apply common sense. I am pragmatic. There are times I've voted for a Democrat because I liked that person's policies more than the other person's policies. But I have mostly voted Republican, because I better relate to most of that party's values — not all of them, however.

I recently gave a book to a prominent Republican here in Florida. It was about how immigrants shaped America. I said, "Read it. Read about the Irish. Read about the Poles. Read about the Germans. Read about the Jews. Read about the Mexicans and the Cubans." Aside from the Native Americans, we are a country of immigrants and, as such, these new arrivals are crucial to the future of our economy and to our growth.

You want to talk about risk taking? You want to talk about job creation? Let me tell you about the man or woman who lives in a little village or is a surgeon or an engineer in Mexico, Ecuador, Venezuela or any other country.

There he is, surrounded by a family, but he chooses to go to North Dakota to work in snow up to his head so he can clean chicken coops and send money back home to take care of his family as a new life or a new business is built in a new homeland. *That's* a risk-taker. We should embrace these people and give them an opportunity to become part of our system and contribute to our values because *that* is the future of America.

Embrace them and their children and treat them like they're going to be the future of America, because they are going to be the future.

Let us all be more accepting and less

Castro poster at Holguin airport, Cuba. Beware of false idols.

ideological. Our own Census tracts point to a slower growth rate among the U.S.-born population. We need these immigrants to help us fund our social programs. We need them to be job creators. Our country's demographics already have changed, and we can't turn the clock back. Our future is greatly dependent on the incoming tide. Let us develop a rational immigration policy, or we will go the way of the Roman Empire.

And, so, here is where I stand:

I believe that each of us is responsible for our own lives, our own moral and ethical compasses, our own success or failure in the world and in life.

I believe we have a profound responsibility to each other. As Americans, we have a responsibility to provide not equality of income or even of living standards, but, yes, *equality of opportunity*.

I believe every American must have the *opportunity* to make the most of his or her inherent intelligence, skills and talent. Nutrition, healthcare, education, the love of caring parents or others, the basics, but high-quality basics — these should be available to all.

"I WAS GIVEN ALL THE OPPORTUNITY THAT AMERICA AFFORDS AND I HAVE DONE WHAT I COULD WITH IT."

This is not *radical*. To me, it is quintessentially American. Give me an opportunity, a chance, and let's see what I can do with it.

Which is why I have written this book.

I was given all the opportunity that America affords, and I have done what I could with it. I did not earn a college degree. I don't think I even have a very high IQ. But the United States gave me a chance to deploy the assets I possessed — drive, a capacity for hard work, endurance and so on.

For that, I am so deeply grateful. As I consider this sense of gratitude and I adjust the angles at which I peer at it, what I see colors my life just as a prism colors light.

I have never forgotten my humble beginnings and those of my parents and their parents. I have never forgotten the work ethic instilled in me by my family. I have never forgotten the most important lessons I learned in school — lessons about living a life of integrity.

The whole point of this book, the whole point of my life now and going forward, is that I realize how fortunate I have been and I realize how grateful I am and must remain. *I want to be remembered for what I have given; not for what I have taken.*

I hope and pray that I somehow can influence my children, my grandchildren and others to feel, appreciate and importantly share their own sense of gratitude for this nation we share, the people we love and the lives we are living.

Each day is unique.

We will never experience this day again.

Today is a gift.

Let's use it wisely — and with generosity.

"In hammock heaven after a horse ride. It's important to be generous to yourself, too."

OCTOBER 22

Outside Sarria

Somewhere between Triacastela and Sarria, I again came across the woman with the green fluorescent backpack. Her name is Helen and I learned more about her.

Helen had started to walk El Camino a year earlier, in 2012, and had made it just past Sarria when she called home, only to be told that her mother had unexpectedly died. Consequently, Helen could not finish her journey to Santiago de Compostela, instead taking a train back to her home in France.

Shortly after her mother's burial, Helen was diagnosed with a terminal cancer, and she was determined to do the walk from Saint-Jean-Pied-de-Port to Santiago de Compostela, her last journey in this life. When she told Jack and me that "I left my broken heart at the Iron Cross," what she meant was that she did not think that she could make it to the top of that mountain, hence finish her journey, until we appeared, and helped her by carrying her backpack.

The lesson — reinforced by Helen's statement — is that we should never let the opportunity pass us by when we can help someone.

Though saddened by Helen's experience, I also had fond memories of the day's destination, Sarria. This was where Michelle and I started our initial El Camino journey the previous May.

As Michelle and I arrived at Rectoral de Goian just north of Sarria, we recognized that finally we were just one day from starting our adventure. We would stay with the family living at the former rectory. This charming 18th-century, stone-walled country inn had been beautifully

"Back in May 2013, after my daughter Michelle's and my first 62-mile walk from Sarria to Santiago de Compostela, it was tough to make the last third of that distance. We were soaked and cold. 'Let's get a ride,' I suggested. Michelle replied: 'We started walking. We will finish walking.' And that was that."

restored. It was here that we would get our first "stamp" in the Pilgrims' Passport.

A terrific memory. Places can represent good and bad memories, to the same person.

But that was then and this is now. The horrendous rain and the howling wind will not subside. The trail is becoming too dangerous, too clogged by mud. When I make Sarria later today, I will consider the journey complete, as between the segment in May and this month-long trek, I have covered the entire 508-mile pilgrimage.

This has been the trip of a lifetime. It accomplished much, and not only for the children for whom we raised millions of dollars.

We helped a terminally ill German woman carry her backpack to the Iron Cross, and then heard her words: "I can go now, as I left my broken heart at the Cross."

We met an autistic young lady who wanted to collect as many "likes" as possible on Facebook.

We helped that taxi driver and her family out of financial crisis by buying them a car they could use as a taxi and make a living from in their small town. I asked her, "What would you do if you had your own taxi?" Her reply was, "I would work all year to change my life." Today, she has her taxi, largely because I was there for other reasons.

We met two nurses from Madrid who walked to give thanks for being allowed to use their training to help others.

Remember that Spanish child I read about who had a serious health problem? Well, we helped her, too, and she received care.

I could go on, but my point is this:

I had a job to do here along the Camino and there in Miami.

That job is done. For now.

"The Pilgrims' Passport from my 62-mile, earlier-in-the-year walk with daughter Michelle. It's worn out from being in my pocket — and stamped at stopping points along the journey."

Chapter 12

This has been a journey that has required more than physical strength. Most of the challenge has been mind over matter.

Near the end of the trip: "Santiago de Compostela is within sight."

ACKNOWLEDGMENTS

In all honesty, I was reluctant to write this story as I felt it would be interpreted as "self-promotion" or seen as an "ego trip." The process of getting comfortable with the idea took years to play out and it had a specific turning point. I wanted to share my values with my children and my family, but I did not recognize the importance that it could acquire in the future until we shared a particular family vacation.

I have always enjoyed the sea — having been born on an island might have something to do with that. For some time, we have kept a boat in Europe, where we would spend the summer months cruising from country to country. It was like having a five-star hotel under us, regardless of where we were.

About 10 years ago, the captain and a crew of 11 kept the family moving from port to port. On a side note, since I only have one daughter, and since boats are always referred to as "she," all my boats have been named after her. This particular boat was Lady Michelle.

So, we were cruising from northern Greece, past Montenegro and into Croatian waters. Once docked in Croatia, I asked my wonderful wife, Constance, about her heritage. I knew that she was born in Michigan of Croatian, Macedonian and Serbian grandparents. I wanted to arrange a visit to the area where her ancestors lived, but to my surprise she did not know. All her knowledge about her past began with her grandparents living just outside Detroit.

After leaving Croatia, we arrived in Venice and, as families do, we explored this historical jewel with my children (Cristofer, my youngest, had not been born yet). That night, as we sat on the third level looking at the Venetian skyline and hearing water taxis zip by, Constance said: "Your children should get to know more about you than I ever got to know about my family before they came to America."

I immediately dismissed the idea, but she persisted, year after year. The more she came to know and love my parents, the more frequently she would bring it up. As time passed, others also brought up the subject — family, people who I worked with, friends and community leaders.

But credit for the genesis of this labor of remembrance belongs to Constance, with a supporting cast of dear friends such as Cesar Alvarez, Dave Lawrence and Eduardo Padrón. They have my deepest thanks and my most profound appreciation and love.

I'd also like to thank David for his "quarterbacking" of this book and for his friendship throughout. Thanks also go to Martin Merzer for helping me put my thoughts on paper, and to Bob Morris and his staff at Story Farm for their fine work in designing this book and shepherding it through the publication and printing process.

An almost-final word: I am not doing this because of a potential financial reward.

I am doing this as a gesture of appreciation to my parents, my wife, the rest of my family, my friends, my business colleagues, and a dear and now departed priest, Father Vincent Duminuco.

I hope that this work will prove beneficial to my children, my grandchildren and those dependents to follow, whom I may never get to know.

Finisterre: "The place the Romans called the end of the then known civilized world. After El Camino passes through Santiago de Compostela — and if you have the energy — you can walk for another five-plus days to this point. (I took a taxi. I was eager to go home. Mission accomplished.)"

I have been humbled by this journey – this journey through life.